A Journey into
Michelangelo's Rome

Angela K. Nickerson

ARTPLACE SERIES

Roaring Forties Press
Berkeley, California

Roaring Forties Press
1053 Santa Fe Avenue
Berkeley, California 94706

ISBN 978-0977742912

Library of Congress Cataloging-in-Publication Data
Nickerson, Angela K., 1973-
  A journey into Michelangelo's Rome / Angela K. Nickerson.
     p. cm. -- (Artplace series)
  Includes bibliographical references and index.
  ISBN 978-0-9777429-1-2 (pbk. : alk. paper)
  1. Michelangelo Buonarroti, 1475-1564. 2. Artists--Italy--Biography. 3.
Rome (Italy)--Description and travel. I. Title.
  N6923.B9N534 2008
  709.2--dc22
  [B]

                                                            2007046792

Per Romano
Mille grázie, mio amore

Contents

Acknowledgments

When I married a Roman in 1998, I had no idea that I was also marrying a city, but that is indeed what happened. My first trip to Rome in 2001 with Romano was one of discovery and true love. As we sat in the Colosseum, Romano sketching and the sun setting, I knew that I would never truly leave. And then, as I stood in the Sistine Chapel, a magnificent creation that I had long heard about and studied, my life changed permanently. I was awestruck.

When Roaring Forties Press put out a call for book proposals, I doubt they expected to hear from someone like me. But they took a chance on someone untested and green. For that, I am profoundly thankful. Nigel Quinney and Deirdre Greene's mentoring, patience, and constant encouragement have made me a better writer and editor.

I owe many thanks to Dr. William Wallace. His understanding of Michelangelo's spirituality encouraged me to explore the topic myself, giving this book a rounder, fuller dimension.

My colleagues and friends at St. John's Lutheran Church were unfailingly supportive and curious. Pastor Scot Sorensen embraced the wireless culture, allowing me to fulfill my work commitments while halfway around the world.

Gregory Favre read the manuscript and in subtle tones encouraged me to abandon the dictum of teaching (say everything five times in five different ways). Through his encouragement, I learned to trust my own voice and my readers as well.

To all of those teachers, including Pat Grisak, Jane Robbins, Steve Swanson, and Diana Postlethwaite, who shaped my writing and taught me the mechanics and ethics of research: thank you. Thanks also to my grandparents, who grew up in tiny Midwestern towns, went on to become citizens of the world, and then taught their grandchildren to do the same. Traveling is like writing: it takes time and practice to do it well. I attribute the gypsy in me to their influence.

I found friends all over the city of Rome. Dr. Irene Iacopi and Maurizio Rulli, as well as the staff at the Soprintendenza Archeologica di Roma, were exceedingly helpful. Padre Luigi Mezzadri at San Silvestro al Quirinale guided me to the balcony where Michelangelo and Vittoria Colonna spent so many hours talking. And everywhere I went, the people of Rome—from the singing cab drivers to the flirtatious policemen—welcomed me and helped me along the way.

My family sustained me day to day. My mom, who traveled with me as my "research assistant," deserves a medal for listening to my incessant prattle as we sprinted from church to museum. My sister, Lisa, listened too, and always asked questions. My dad sent me hilarious e-mails and kept me laughing through the stomach flu and stolen luggage. Sincere thanks also to the rest of my family and friends, who made me feel like a celebrity and who have vowed to buy a zillion copies of this book.

But truly it is my husband, Romano, who deserves the most thanks. He did the laundry and the dishes and cooked and cleaned and gardened for months on end while I worked. He explained the mysteries of building domes and reassured me that cutting the manuscript in half was actually a good thing. And his memories of camping on the beach at Ostia and romping through the ruins took us back to the Italy of his childhood.

Martin Luther wrote of the connection between education and vocation, insisting that through education we discover our gifts, which we then should use for the greater good. Michelangelo believed much the same, finding holiness and spiritual connection in the ring of chisel against marble. This book represents a fusion of art, literature, spirituality, history, and travel—the things about which I am most passionate. When my mother took me to an exhibit about Pompeii as a child . . . when my father read *Tom Sawyer* to me at night . . . when my teachers encouraged my passion for the Pre-Raphaelites . . . when my grandparents took me to the USSR . . . they were all equipping me for this project and helping me to discover my own gifts.

I am so blessed to have been given this vocation.

A Journey into
Michelangelo's
Rome

Chapter 1
The Meaning of Perfection
Michelangelo and His Times

Michelangelo's work in the Sistine Chapel is today revered as an icon of the Renaissance but provoked controversy at the time.

On March 6, 1475, Michelangelo Buonarroti was born to poor aristocrats in Caprese, near Florence. Barely thirty years later, he was hailed throughout Italy and much of Europe as one of the greatest artists of all time, a judgment of which he was keenly aware and that he would bemoan yet try to preserve throughout his life.

Michelangelo's artistic contributions redefined Rome as the self-proclaimed "capital of the world." In turn, the world celebrated the artist for his redefinition of beauty and expression, reclaiming the word "genius"—a term resurrected from the Latin—to describe this singular artist's talents. Michelangelo's contemporaries struggled to describe the phenomenal talents of a man whose work surpassed all superlatives. According to one of Michelangelo's friends and biographers, Giorgio Vasari, God sent "to earth a spirit who, working alone, was able to demonstrate in every art and every profession the meaning of perfection." Although many artists fade from popularity as styles and tastes change, Michelangelo's golden reputation has never tarnished. More than five hundred years since his death, visitors still flock to see the frescoes, sculptures, and architecture with which Michelangelo adorned Rome.

A New Italy

The world into which Michelangelo was born was in the midst of a cultural and intellectual revolution, a revolution that Michelangelo's contemporaries called the *rinascita* and that we know as the Renaissance. Today, the Renaissance—which swept Europe from the fourteenth to the seventeenth centuries—is probably best known for its innovations in art. But the artistic leaps of the Renaissance did not happen in a vacuum. They arose within a maelstrom of enormously potent political, economic, and social change. In Italy, the winds of change transformed a collection of warring principalities and city-states into the continent's mercantile and cultural powerhouse.

The seeds of the Renaissance germinated in the grimmest of soils: the Black Death. The pandemic of bubonic plague that Italian merchants unwittingly brought to Europe from Asia in 1348 quickly swept over the Italian peninsula and then the rest of Europe, leaving millions dead and opening the door to poverty and war. In the wake of the Black Death,

The Black Death of the mid-1300s killed 20–30 million people in Europe, between one-third and one-half of the entire population.

the city-states and kingdoms of Florence, Pisa, Milan, Naples, and Venice battled one another for dominance, while Rome, once indomitable, fell from contention. The papacy, the single wealthiest and most powerful force on the peninsula, was riven by division and moved from Rome to France.

But by the mid-1400s, despite the continued clashes between city-states, the environment on the peninsula had changed markedly. The papacy had returned to Rome, bringing with it a moneyed, cultured, and educated population. Venice had emerged as the center of the shipping and ship-building industries and become a gateway for the vigorous flow of money and goods in and out of Italy. Italy had established itself as Europe's door to the Middle East and Asia.

The known world was expanding as European explorers discovered new lands. Christopher Columbus landed on the coast of North America. Vasco da Gama navigated around the Cape of Good Hope. Cortéz accomplished his bloody conquest of Mexico, and the Spanish conquered Brazil. The Portuguese acquainted themselves with Japan. Intellectually, horizons were being expanded as well: in 1513, Machiavelli, an exiled Florentine, wrote *The Prince*, a treatise on how to acquire and retain political power that achieved widespread fame because of a new technology—the printing press, which allowed all sorts of ideas, including the notion of religious rebellion, to race across Europe.

As trade flourished and navigation improved, geographic and political boundaries between East and West blurred, and the rich, spicy world of the Middle East infused Italian culture. Europe exported bulky goods like wool, timber, and semiprecious metals. In exchange, ships packed with luxuries returned, profoundly changing the Renaissance diet, wardrobe, and decoration. Spices and fabrics, plants and pigments, precious metals and jewels came to Italy from around the Mediterranean: Muslim Spain, Egypt, Turkey, and Persia. Soaps, sandalwood, and opium became popular. Dried fruits, salts, cloves, nutmeg, black pepper, and

Ciambue's *Santa Trinita Madonna* (c. 1280).

Renaissance Artists

Italians recognized the extraordinary circumstances under which they thrived. In the sixteenth century, they used the term *rinascita* to refer to the revival of classical culture. The word "renaissance," from the French word meaning "rebirth," was not used until the nineteenth century.

Art historians still follow the classifications invented by Giorgio Vasari, who identified three periods of Renaissance art. Looking at the art that surrounded him, Vasari saw the beginning of the cultural rebirth with *i primi lumi* (the first lights) that appeared in the fourteenth century. Known today as the "Pre-Renaissance," this period is best known for the rediscovery of the principle of forced perspective in painting as well as a return to realism. Vasari points to Giotto and Cimabue as the finest artists of this period.

Art from the Early Renaissance (roughly, the fifteenth century), epitomized by Brunelleschi's dome in Florence, shows a technical mastery and use of color that creates even more realism. Additionally, Early Renaissance artists were keenly aware of and influenced by ancient Rome and Greece. Donatello created the first nude sculpture since antiquity. Ghiberti and Masaccio created masterpieces that would profoundly influence those who came after them—the artists of the High Renaissance.

Michelangelo, da Vinci, and Raphael are the archetypical artists of the High Renaissance. In the sixteenth century, they perfected the use of color, perspective, and proportion and applied these tools to human and humanist subjects. The influence of the ancients was strong among the artists of the High Renaissance, but no principle was more important than Protagoras's idea that "man is the measure of all things." Anatomy, proportion, symmetry, and perspective permeated architecture, painting, sculpture, poetry, and music.

Italy in the sixteenth century.

cinnamon found their way into rich dishes and baked goods served on tables laden with gilded glassware and precious porcelain. Ostentation and opulence became commonplace.

A New Appreciation for Antiquity

The flow of goods created a thriving merchant class across the peninsula. Flush with disposable income, these merchants and their families hungered for prestige and came to believe that the path to social advancement was paved with social grace. So they spent much of the leisure time their wealth afforded them on self-improvement, especially on reading the writings of ancient Greek and Roman poets, historians, and philosophers. The concept of the "magnificent man," as originally formulated by one of those philosophers, Aristotle, came back into vogue:

> The magnificent man is like an artist; for he can see what is fitting and spend large sums tastefully . . . a magnificent man spends not on himself but on public objects. . . . [he] will also furnish his house suitably to his wealth (for even a house is a sort of public ornament), and will spend by preference on those works that are lasting (for these are the most beautiful).

Inspired by Aristotle, Italians embraced the notion of *l'uomo universale*, the complete man (or, as we would put it today, the Renaissance man). *L'uomo universale* appreciated the arts and could speak knowledgeably about music, painting, architecture, and sculpture. He had refined tastes and manners, and was masculine and athletic. He was educated in the teachings of writers such as Dante, Boccaccio, and Aquinas as well as history and the texts of antiquity. In addition, *l'uomo universale* enjoyed decorating his home and his person with fine, rare, and expensive things, for the world of the wealthy was one of lush refinement. The Italian *nouveau riche*—and even the aristocrats they so envied—strove to behave like the "magnificent man."

As antique sculptures were discovered in the fifteenth and sixteenth centuries, the papacy would take them and place them in the Vatican for contemporary artists to study. The *Belvedere Torso* inspired many Renaissance artists.

This detail of a fresco created in 1441–2 by Domenico di Bartolo captures the Renaissance zeal for both perspective and luxuriant colors and materials.

New smells, textures, colors, and tastes saturated the senses, and *l'uomo universale* found art in all aspects of life. Gradually, artistic beauty was demanded in everything from home décor to tailoring, furniture to frescoes. A fascination with antiquity emerged, resurrecting the power of ancient texts, ideas, sculpture, and architecture and transforming the entire Italian peninsula, especially two cities: Florence and Rome.

As artists in Renaissance Italy rediscovered the skills of the ancients, they awakened a fervor for the arts that catapulted their profession into the public eye. The public did not adopt the ancients' attitudes toward artists themselves, however. The ancients had seen painting and sculpture as mere crafts performed by laborers; vestiges of this idea persisted through the Middle Ages. During the Renaissance, the affluent and the powerful in Italy engaged in bidding wars for the services of Italy's greatest artists— among whom Michelangelo would soon be counted.

Like the ancient Romans, Renaissance artists tended to work in workshops, pooling resources under a strict master-apprentice system. In 1478, when

Michelangelo was just three years old, Florence had a population of sixty thousand people. That population supported fifty-four workshops of sculptors, forty-four of goldsmiths, and forty of painters, according to guild records. Work was plentiful, and even peasants with talent were able to find sponsors.

As the wealthy competed for the services of the best artists, the artists competed among themselves for the most-renowned masters, the fattest commissions, and the loudest acclaim. They became faster, more prolific, and better at their craft, imitating and innovating at every turn.

A New Way of Seeing

Michelangelo embarked upon his artistic career at the height of this frenzy. As the sixteenth century dawned and he came into manhood, wealth and opportunity swirled about him. Treasure hunters actively combed Roman ruins for masterpieces of Greco-Roman sculpture. The long-abandoned ruins of the Empire became classrooms for budding and blossomed artists alike. For painters, not only were there greater opportunities to paint, but the color palette also expanded with the importation of lapis lazuli, vermilion, and cinnabar, creating velvety rich colors for frescoists.

In 1490, an ancient Greek sculpture of Apollo was discovered in an Italian villa; the *Belvedere Torso*, as it soon became known, was instantly revered as a specimen of unparalleled aesthetic majesty. Artists looked to ancient buildings—better preserved than they are today—and studied the classical orders of architecture and other ancient principles of construction. They admired the unity of classical designs and emulated the fine craftsmanship that allowed the structures to withstand a millennium or more of neglect.

Bella Figura
Roman women today are known for dressing with ease and grace. Men, too, spend time and money on their toilette and their clothing. Romans would never, for example, wear running shoes except when going running.

The Italian concept of dressing well, of presenting a *bella figura*, reaches back to the Renaissance and a time when the body was used to display wealth and exotic goods—much as it is today. The houses of Fendi and Ferragamo, Valentino and Armani all owe their roots to the grandiosity and extravagance of the Renaissance.

The achievements of Renaissance artists were many: the mastery of landscape, the use of vivid colors, the rediscovery of the nude, the portrait as an art form. But the use of perspective and its mathematical principles sets the art of the period apart. It allowed

Good Manners
In an effort to correct his fellow Romans' manners, Giovanni della Casa (1503–56) wrote an influential treatise in 1555 called *Il Galateo*. In it he prescribed good manners and proper deportment—not just in royal or courtly circumstances, but also in everyday situations. The work of this Miss Manners of Renaissance Rome survives in the Italian phrase *sapere il galateo*. Translated as "to know the Galateo," it describes someone with impeccable manners.

artists to achieve a greater level of realism than had been seen in Europe since ancient times.

Although Renaissance artists imitated their predecessors, they also brought a new depth to art that eluded the anonymous artists of the ancient world. It is said that the ancients conveyed life in their art, but Michelangelo and his contemporaries brought souls to their figures. As they pushed to differentiate their works from those of their competitors, the Renaissance artists broke new emotional ground, depicting the solitude, tension, suffering, and strife of the human condition in vivid and unprecedented ways. Art, too, became an expression of social and religious ideas, inspiring the faithful but also stirring up controversy.

A Tale of Two Cities

Michelangelo spent almost all of his life in two very different cities. Walking the streets of Rome and Florence today, a visitor immediately sees the differences between the Eternal City and her northern cousin. Rome is a mosaic of ancient ruins, Renaissance splendors, Fascist monuments, and postmodern buildings. The streets reflect centuries of tumult, wealth, poverty, growth, contraction, and instability. In contrast, Florence looks much as she did five centuries ago. Her streets, narrow and cobbled, are lined with neat and tidy shops and apartments and illustrate the sensibilities of a city where beauty and order reigned. Florence thrived from the early days of the Renaissance, while Rome languished until the return of the pope in 1420. And whereas Florence fashioned herself as the seat of civilized gentility, Rome was a city of turmoil, greed, power, and money. In his medieval allegory, *The Decameron,* Boccaccio (1313–75) describes Romans as "avaricious and grasping after money" and says that "for money they bought and sold human, and even Christian, blood, and also every sort of divine thing."

This engraving of Michelangelo's design for the Campidoglio in Rome was made by Étienne Dupérac in 1568.

Michelangelo appears to have shared Boccaccio's opinion—certainly, the experience of living in Rome made him long for Florence. Yet, he spent more of his life in Rome, it was in Rome that he formed his most intimate friendships, and it was in Rome that he created the lion's share of his masterpieces.

A Journey into Michelangelo's Rome

Because Florence rightfully claims Michelangelo as her native son, this book begins there, charting his birth and background, his artistic training and first commissions, and his relationships with a colorful family and a powerful patron. Yet, like Michelangelo, this book soon switches location and moves to Rome. Most chapters focus on a major work Michelangelo undertook while in that city of papal wealth and grand commissions. From the acclaim that greeted the unveiling of his *Pietà* in 1499 to the moral condemnation that was heaped in 1541 upon his frescoes for the Sistine Chapel, from the protracted controversy surrounding the design and construction of St. Peter's Basilica to the artist's equally lengthy but almost secretive efforts to complete the tomb of Pope Julius II, *A Journey into Michelangelo's Rome* tells a story of intrigue, passion, perseverance, and a developing

faith. It is a story, too, that allows the reader to traverse the city, stopping at the Forum and the Colosseum, witnessing weddings at the Campidoglio, visiting bustling markets in the Piazza Navona, and

Ascanio Condivi described Michelangelo as "well built; his body tends more to nerves and bones than to flesh and fat, healthy above all."

St. Peter's Basilica from Ponte Sant' Angelo.

enjoying the quiet of Santa Maria sopra Minerva, before turning up Via della Conciliazione to admire the majestic dome of St. Peter's.

This book presents a portrait of the artist not just as a public figure but also as a private man. Most educated Westerners identify the frescoes of the Sistine Chapel with their creator. The image of God and Adam, arms outstretched and nearly touching, has come to represent the genius of an artist and the wealth of talent that once populated Rome. The perception of Michelangelo as a suffering and temperamental artist dates back to his own time. In this myth, retold and embellished, the artist has become a figure larger than life and barely recognizable.

But just as the Sistine Chapel's frescoes are ultimately two-dimensional representations of an idea, so too is the image of the suffering genius a simplistic view of a complicated man. Michelangelo may have relished the power his reputation afforded, and he was certainly proud of his accomplishments, quick to take offense, and often slow to forgive, but he was a very sensitive and affectionate man, devoted to his family, protective of his servants, and loyal to his friends.

As he worked on his masterpieces, Michelangelo gathered his friends together, including his confidantes, Vittoria Colonna and Tommaso de' Cavalieri, and his faithful assistant, Urbino. Through his friendships, he explored the shadows and doubts of his deepening faith. Surrounded by the trappings of papal power, Michelangelo wrestled with the questions posed by the Reformation. His theological struggles were reflected in his sculpture, the unambiguous emotional power of his *Pietà* giving way to increasingly pensive works, both public and private.

Although he considered himself first and foremost a sculptor, Michelangelo was forced to take on the roles of frescoist and architect as well. Political and financial considerations dictated that this intensely private man had to produce enormous public works. He reshaped the Capitoline Hill, the seat of Roman power and history. He redefined the Sistine Chapel, the seat of papal politics and continuity. And he sculpted the dome of St. Peter's, transforming the Roman skyline and fusing the grace of the ancients with the might of the Vatican.

In his private life, Michelangelo wrote. Littered among the half-finished marbles, chisels, and stones in his workshop were scraps of paper on which he composed poetry as well as grocery lists. He wrote to others about the frustration of dealing with capricious popes who often proved reluctant to pay for what they had commissioned. He regularly corresponded with friends, acquaintances, and family members, generating a record of his feuds, joys, and griefs. *A Journey into Michelangelo's Rome* draws upon this trove of writings, as well as upon the better-known artistic record, to tell the story of how, amid the ruins of the Roman Empire and the largesse of the Vatican, Michelangelo the Florentine found ancient inspiration, created ageless beauty, and earned the enduring love and respect of Romans.

In 1564, when Michelangelo died, Rome grieved deeply. From then to now, he has been honored and celebrated by a city with a long memory and a rich past. Romans consider themselves experts on their adopted son. They name their streets, their hotels, their restaurants, and even their children for the man who shaped their city half a millennium ago. *A Journey into Michelangelo's Rome* explores this city, this man, and the world that shaped them both.

Chapter 2
Florence
Michelangelo and the House of Medici

Finished in 1434, the dome over Santa Maria del Fiore dominates the skyline of Florence. Having grown up in its shadow, Michelangelo drew on it as a precedent for his dome over St. Peter's Basilica in Rome.

Michelangelo was born in 1475 to parents living in genteel poverty. The family lived in Caprese near Florence, where Michelangelo's father, Lodovico di Leonardo Buonarroti Simoni, had a minor government appointment. His mother, Francesca Neri di Miniato del Sera, fell from a horse during her pregnancy; happily, the fall did not seem to affect the child she was carrying.

Lodovico had married Francesca a few years before, in 1472, when she was about seventeen and he was twenty-seven. The proud father wrote of his son's birth:

> I record that on this day the sixth of March 1475 a son was born to me: I gave him the name of Michelangelo, and he was born on Monday morning, before four or five o'clock, and he was born to me while I was podestà of Caprese, and he was born at Caprese: the godfathers were those named below. He was baptized on the eighth day of the same month in the church of San Giovanni at Caprese.

15

As was typical for a child from his social class, Michelangelo was sent to live with a wet nurse for his first few years. The nurse was the daughter and the wife of stonemasons, leading Michelangelo to jokingly declare, "If I have any intelligence at all, it has come . . . because I took the hammer and chisels with which I carve my figures from my wet-nurse's milk."

Michelangelo had four siblings: one older brother, Leonardo, and three younger ones, Buonarroto, Giovansimone, and Gismondo. Their mother died in 1481, the year Gismondo was born. Michelangelo's sensitive images of women with their children—from the *Rome Pieta* to the mothers on the ceiling of the Sistine Chapel—reflect the longing of a boy who was motherless from the age of six.

Michelangelo's portrayals of women were also shaped by the rich beauty of his hometown; Florence in the fifteenth century was a city of prosperity, elegance, and artistry. From Ghiberti's bronze doors on the baptistry of Santa Maria del Fiore depicting detailed friezes of Biblical stories, which Michelangelo would call "the Gates of Paradise," to Brunelleschi's dome and della Robbia's medallions on the Ospedale degli Innocenti, the city through which young Michelangelo wandered was filled with art on public display. After all, the Medici family had planned it that way.

The Medici Family

For all intents and purposes, the Medici family ruled Florence during the fifteenth century. Officially, the city-state was a republican oligarchy ruled by the Signoria. This council comprising nine citizens chosen by lots every two months was composed of the *gonfaloniere* of justice, a man chosen as the standard bearer for the Republic, and eight *priori*. However, the Medici family wielded its power to rig drawings in its

favor, buying the loyalties of any eligible man they could. And the public, by and large, did not object. In fact, most Florentines were content to have the Medici in charge.

The Medici fortunes came from the banking industry. The Florentine gold florin had established itself during the Middle Ages as one of Europe's major currencies. Whereas Venice's economy flourished because of sea trade, Florence's grew due to her industry—wool and cloth production—and an intricate international commercial network developed during the Middle Ages. The funds flowing in and out of the city required bankers, and the Medici family became the most prominent banking family in Europe. Cosimo the Elder (1389–1464) and Lorenzo (1449–92), both brilliant statesmen and brutal strategists, wielded their power firmly but fairly and fostered a culture of loyalty and economic stability that allowed them to rule Florence for nearly a century.

The Medici were not the only family of prominence in fifteenth-century Florence, however. The Strozzi, Pitti, Pazzi, and Capponi families also had large fortunes and were active political players. They too funded great art projects, and with so many fortunes devoted to public beautification, Florence became a city of visual drama and the seat of good taste.

Florence's pantheon of celebrated artists includes talents from many genres and media. In designing and raising the dome over Santa Maria del Fiore—or, as it is known, Il Duomo—Brunelleschi built the largest dome since antiquity, a marvel completed in 1434 (just forty-one years before Michelangelo's birth). Giotto, a celebrated frescoist, designed the bell tower at the same church, and Ghiberti designed the bronze doors for the church's baptistry. The city's churches, public spaces, and private homes were adorned by sculptor Donatello;

Santa Maria del Fiore's dome impresses with its scale, but a stunning, smaller masterpiece adorns the east entrance to the baptistry. Ghiberti's doors, created between 1425 and 1452, feature ten small panels. Each panel vividly illustrates an Old Testament story. The doors on display today are reproductions of the originals, which were moved inside to the Museo dell'Opera del Duomo (just to the east of Il Duomo) so that they would be protected from the elements.

by painters Cimabue, Fra Angelico, Botticelli, and Masaccio; and, by the ultimate in versatility, Leonardo da Vinci, who wrote books, painted canvases, and designed a helicopter, among hundreds of other inventions.

Not only did the Florentine atmosphere cultivate visual artists, it also fostered writers who followed in the footsteps of Dante, fourteenth-century creator of the *Divine Comedy*. Poets Petrarch and Boccaccio joined the political philosopher Machiavelli and art historian Vasari on the list of Florence's greatest sons. Their works became enormously popular in large part because of a technological revolution—the printing press—and an intellectual movement—humanism.

The Printing Press

The Vatican Library, now considered one of the finest and most exclusive collections in the world, consisted in 1420 of just three hundred volumes. Soon thereafter, fifteenth-century Italy was consumed by a manuscript-collecting craze. Manuscripts, chiefly texts by Greek and Roman philosophers, were copied by hand in monasteries across Europe and became highly prized. The wealthy and learned competed to acquire the most beautiful manuscripts as pieces of art as well as symbols of knowledge. Pope Nicholas V (1447–55), an avid collector of manuscripts, ransacked monastic libraries in search of ancient Greek and Latin texts.

In 1450, an invention in a small town in Germany would redirect this bibliophilic fervor and prove to be the most influential invention of the Renaissance: the printing press. The first printing press arrived in Rome by 1465; soon thereafter, the ancient texts so treasured in Italy were being printed cheaply and efficiently in Italy itself.

A sixteenth-century image of a printing office showing the compositor, the printers, and the proofreader at work.

To illustrate the dramatic impact of the printing press, consider this: forty-five scribes could, under ideal conditions, produce a maximum of one hundred manuscripts in a one-year period. The first printing press in Rome, run by two Germans, Sweynheym and Pannartz, printed twelve thousand books in its first five years of production. By the 1480s, there were more than one hundred presses in Italy.

By 1500, fifteen million books had been printed in Europe—more than the sum total of all manuscripts produced in the preceding millennium. In the sixteenth century, more than 150 million books were published in England alone, a country with a population of only four million people. Suddenly, a library of three hundred volumes looked a bit small.

The first printed books were religious in nature: Bibles, sermons, and catechisms. Before long, the presses were printing secular books, including editions by classical authors such as Aristotle, Socrates, and Cato. In 1530, a printed pamphlet cost the same as a loaf of bread. A copy of the New Testament cost the equivalent of a laborer's daily wage. A literary—and a literate—culture emerged.

Religious books were initially published in Latin or Greek, the languages of the church, but texts soon appeared in the vernacular languages of the day—languages for which standardized forms of spelling, grammar, and punctuation did not exist. Over time, the language of the people became as standardized and codified as the language of the clergy. Trade, politics, and business had all once been conducted in Latin or Greek, but eventually vernacular languages were used in these exchanges, too.

The dissemination of ideas through printed text shaped the Renaissance. Part of a gentleman's training in Renaissance Italy was an education in the works of antiquity. Now educators were able to market new ways of learning and study to an eager public. Politicians and theologians sought to sway opinion with a torrent of tracts, treatises, and pamphlets.

A Humanist Education

Around the time of his mother's death, Michelangelo started school, but he was a reluctant student. He was tutored by a humanist scholar, Francesco Galatea of Urbino. Humanism, an intellectual movement that grew out of an increasing demand for intellectuals in the changing Italian economy, spawned hundreds of small private schools devoted to educating the merchant class and the children of the working nobility. Rooted in the studies of ancient Greek and Roman texts, humanism flourished as the printing press made texts widely available.

A humanist education offered two things. First, so the humanists claimed, those who read and understood the classics were more moral and made wiser decisions. Second, students could learn the skills needed to become lawyers, politicians, or priests. Harkening back to the ideals of ancient Rome, the humanists regarded service as the perfect employment for an educated and thoughtful populace.

At school, Michelangelo studied the classic texts. Students first would read a text in the original Latin or Greek. Then they would translate the text into Italian—a task that measured true comprehension. Students also learned letter writing and public speaking, making them employable in a range of fields.

Michelangelo described himself as a poor student who scribbled and drew rather than mastering the Latin grammar before him. "Although he profited somewhat from the study of letters," remarked Michelangelo's biographer and contemporary Ascanio Condivi, "at the same time nature and the heavens, which are so difficult to withstand, were drawing him toward painting; so that he could not resist running off here and there to draw whenever he could steal some time and seeking the company of painters."

Michelangelo's father, Lodovico, was old-fashioned; he didn't want his son to become a painter, which he considered beneath his family's social position. But Lodovico also took great pride in being a distant relation of Lorenzo de' Medici, and Lorenzo, a tremendous patron of the arts, did not consider painting to be a lowly trade. But the fact remained: no Buonarroti had ever been an artist. Both Michelangelo's father and his uncle Francesco beat the young Michelangelo in an effort to change his inclination.

An Apprenticeship

After many battles, Michelangelo's father was finally forced to acknowledge his son's driving passion. Lodovico then approached Lorenzo de' Medici, hoping to secure an apprenticeship for his son. Lorenzo arranged for the young man to apprentice with Domenico Ghirlandaio, a Florentine master frescoist, under a contract that paid Michelangelo substantially more than a normal apprentice.

By the age of thirteen, Michelangelo was working in Ghirlandaio's workshop. According to legend, he was so bored by the drudgery of preparing paints and caring for brushes that he set out to better his master rather than imitate him. At one point, he copied a portrait painted by Ghirlandaio and then switched the copy with the original, a trick the master did not detect.

Michelangelo displayed an intense curiosity and work ethic early on. As a young pupil, a biographer noted, he would "go off to the fish market, where he observed the shape and coloring of the fins of the fish, the color of the eyes and every other part, and he would render them in his painting."

Like many young, brilliant men, Michelangelo was cocky. One day, Pietro Torrigiano, a fellow apprentice,

During Michelangelo's apprenticeship, Ghirlandaio worked on the Tornabuoni Chapel in Santa Maria Novella. As Ghirlandaio's apprentice, Michelangelo spent most of his time performing routine tasks such as preparing colors. But Michelangelo was also able to work on sketches and to study Ghirlandaio's techniques for dividing space and telling stories through his lifelike figures, such as in *The Nativity of the Virgin*. The relationship between master and apprentice eventually soured, however; in his later years, Michelangelo claimed to have learned nothing from Ghirlandaio.

had had enough. "Buonarroti had the habit of making fun of anyone else who was drawing there, and one day he provoked me so much that I lost my temper more than usual, and, clenching my fist, gave him such a punch on the nose that I felt the bone and cartilage crush like a biscuit. So that fellow will carry my signature till he dies." Indeed, in portraits of him as a grown man, Michelangelo's nose appears somewhat misshapen and flattened.

Michelangelo's apprenticeship with Ghirlandaio did not last the three years intended. He soon captured the attention of Lorenzo de' Medici—with a forgery. Michelangelo carved a small faun, imitating an antiquity, which caught Lorenzo's eye. Jokingly,

Lorenzo told the young man, "Oh, you have made this faun old and left him all his teeth. Don't you know that old men of that age are always missing a few?" When Lorenzo left the room for a few minutes, Michelangelo quickly removed one of the faun's teeth. When Lorenzo returned, he told Michelangelo that he wished to speak with his father and invited Michelangelo to work for him at the Medici Gardens.

Michelangelo and Il Magnifico

Florence was one of the most powerful city-states in Italy due in large part to the presence of the Medici family, "God's bankers," who helped the papacy deploy its wealth across the continent.

Forgery

That Michelangelo was involved in forging antiquities was not remarkable. The fever for antiquities among the art-loving public created a market for forgeries, and most Renaissance sculptors committed forgery to pay the bills, at least until they established their own reputations. Because artists learned to create through imitation, they were well-equipped to create fakes.

One of Michelangelo's projects, a sleeping cupid (now lost), caught the eye of Lorenzo di Pierfrancesco de' Medici, a cousin of the great Lorenzo. Medici suggested that Michelangelo age the sculpture and try to pass it off as an antiquity. He said, "If you buried it, I am convinced it would pass as an ancient work, and if you sent it to Rome treated so that it appeared old, you would earn much more than by selling it here."

Michelangelo agreed to the deception. Accounts are foggy as to what happened next. The sculpture, it seems, was sold to a cardinal in Rome, but Michelangelo was cheated out of his money by his intermediary.

The cardinal discovered that he had been tricked into buying a forgery and demanded his money back. Vasari, Michelangelo's contemporary and his most famous biographer, claims that the cardinal's reputation was damaged because he "did not recognize the value of the work, which consists in its perfection, for modern works are just as good as ancient ones when they are excellent." But Vasari wrote with the benefit of hindsight; in the early days of Michelangelo's career, ancient works were more valued than those of contemporary artists.

In recent years, some scholars have suggested that Michelangelo may have pulled off the greatest forgery of all: the celebrated *Laocoön*. In 1506, Pope Julius II asked Michelangelo and his friend, Giuliano da Sangallo, among others, to identify and authenticate a sculpture that had been discovered in a vineyard near Santa Maria Maggiore. The sculpture was identified as a work described in Pliny's Roman histories from the first century A.D. and lost for more than a millennium; the pope purchased it for an enormous sum. One theory is that Michelangelo, schooled in the art of forgery, carved *Laocoön* during his first trip to Rome and buried it to be "discovered" at a later date.

LAVRENTIVS MEDICES PETRI FILIVS.

Lorenzo de' Medici considered the city of Florence his own personal beautification project. Whether he was securing patrons for artists, arranging marriages, striking financial deals, or sponsoring pageants and carnivals, he aspired to bring beauty to the city. He also saw his civic works as a means to justify the money he made from banking, traditionally regarded as a sinful occupation.

Lorenzo de' Medici, known widely as Il Magnifico, headed the family empire with a keen skill for diplomacy. Taking a page from the Roman emperors' book, Il Magnifico helped to ensure peace and harmony in Florence by keeping the public entertained. He commissioned large-scale art projects and sponsored festivals and pageantry. In doing so, he also funded a flourishing arts community and helped to foster an intensely creative and intellectual environment. Lorenzo loved Dante and wrote sheaves of poetry—both sacred and scandalously sensual. As a poet, he used the Tuscan vernacular, setting a precedent for many Tuscans who put pen to paper, including Michelangelo.

Michelangelo's decision to leave Ghirlandaio's workshop for the Medici Gardens could not have pleased his father, who saw his son leaving one questionable profession for another even more pedestrian. Sculpting was dirty, physical, and exhausting work. Most sculptors were employed in creating decorative elements and architectural embellishments, a trade for commoners.

To Michelangelo, however, nothing was more prestigious than to have Il Magnifico as a patron. The Medici Gardens was not a school with a curriculum or instructors. Rather, it was an informal gathering place for sculptors, philosophers, and poets dedicated to the study of antiquities and classical texts. When Michelangelo arrived at the Medici Gardens, he entered a world of intense intellectual pursuit and political savvy, which he had to navigate with skill. And he found himself riding the coattails of one of the most powerful men in the world.

Michelangelo lived in the Medici house for nearly two years, and he worked on his first two surviving sculptures there. Both *The Battle of the Centaurs* (c. 1491) and *The Madonna of the Stairs* (c. 1489–92) show the

The Palazzo Vecchio overlooks the Piazza della Signoria, where the religous zealot Savonarola and his followers burned "sinful luxuries." Today, a copy of Michelangelo's *David* resides near the same spot where Savonarola himself was burned in 1498.

The Madonna of the Stairs (c. 1489–92).

imagination and skill of a young man who had impeccable classical models to study. As with his academic studies, Michelangelo's artistic instruction consisted largely of imitation. Whether with the brush, the chisel, or the pencil, imitation of works by masters was considered the finest form of instruction. So an apprentice copied the works of his master over and over until he was deemed skillful enough to procure his own work. Michelangelo proved an exemplary mimic.

In 1492, Michelangelo's patron died. The power vacuum created with Lorenzo's death changed Florence irrevocably and set the seventeen-year-old Michelangelo on a course toward Rome. For two generations, the Medici family had ensured peace in Florence by pleasing the public and influencing the city's ruling body, the Signoria. The success of this strategy depended on it being executed with both political cunning and diplomatic activity. Lorenzo's son, Piero, had neither talent.

The Bonfires of the Vanities

Michelangelo cultivated an image of perfection and genius, learning from an early age to destroy pieces he did not deem worthy. Very few sketches remain from his enormous volume of work, and nothing is left from his days as a student. This contributes to the mythical fog shrouding his reputation and bolsters the perception that he was a genius, born not trained.

Michelangelo's proclivity for burning his materials may have stemmed from the influence of Florence's fieriest preacher, Girolamo Savonarola (1452–98). The passionate orator thrived on discontent and disaster, heating up the political climate of the city with his graphic and violent prophecies. When Lorenzo de' Medici died in 1492, Savonarola seized power in the city. Michelangelo, who from a young age had shown intense religious devotion, identified with Savonarola's gloomy vision for mankind and his apocalyptic view. But Michelangelo's admiration for Savonarola was tested by the latter's rejection of the Renaissance, Plato, the value of art, and the influence of the ancients. Savonarola's army of "angels"—children and young men dressed in white robes—roamed the city, informing on their families and neighbors and seizing works of art, lavish clothes, and other items that Savonarola frowned upon.

In the Piazza della Signoria at the center of Florence, Savonarola and his angels built enormous fires—"Bonfires of the Vanities"—into which they threw wigs, perfumes, soaps, playing cards, chessboards, manuscripts, and other luxuries that Savonarola deemed sinful. Such an environment was extraordinarily uncomfortable for the artists of Florence, who fled to Rome and Venice to escape the same fate as their works.

Savonarola's fervor infected Michelangelo, causing him to ponder theological questions long after the bonfires were extinguished. Vasari wrote, "As the admirable Christian he was, Michelangelo took great pleasure from the Holy Scriptures, and he held in great veneration the works written by Fra Girolamo Savonarola, whom he had heard preaching in the pulpit."

In adulthood, Michelangelo's proclivity for destroying his work antagonized his followers, who realized that the work of a celebrity would be valuable someday. It was a habit he maintained to his last days, however. Any doodles, poems, sketches, and letters that betrayed weakness all met a fiery end.

With Lorenzo's death, potent powers in the city-state sensed weakness and pounced. Savonarola, a Dominican priest who had been advocating change and piety from the pulpit, unleashed a torrent of political fury and apocalyptic prophecy. Preaching Old Testament vengeance and disaster, he damned Florence for its decadence and passion for beauty. Ultimately, he would turn on the papacy and the Medici family.

Amid the turmoil, Michelangelo spent the next few years flitting between Florence and her neighbor seventy miles to the north, Bologna, as the fortunes of his patrons rose and fell. Fiercely independent, unlike many of his contemporaries, he refused to join a workshop. But as the artists of Florence fled to Rome and Venice, Michelangelo found himself increasingly alone. He decided it was time to make a change. Il Magnifico's cousin Lorenzo di Pierfrancesco de' Medici wrote some letters of introduction for the young sculptor. Armed with the letters and ready to prove his abilities in a more hospitable environment, Michelangelo set off for Rome.

Chapter 3
Rome
Marvels in Marble

The Roman Forum was the heart of the ancient city and the center of both its political and its religious life. By the time Michelangelo wandered through the ruins, sheep and cattle grazed among the toppled columns and sculptures. As Rome was rebuilt, however, the Forum became a popular place to find building materials. Doors, columns, sculptures, and tons of marble were spirited away from the ruins and recycled in Renaissance buildings all over Rome. Today, it is both a public space for all to enjoy and an active archaeological site.

Civic and religious authority have always mingled in Rome. Since the days when emperors were worshipped as gods, the line between spiritual and earthly powers in Rome has been fuzzy. Indeed, the principles of the empire's organization influenced the organization of the Christian church, with bishops governing dioceses just as Roman governors ruled provinces.

At its peak, the Roman Empire dominated the Mediterranean, the Middle East, Northern Africa, and Europe. The vast size of the empire, however, overstretched Rome's ability to administer and protect it, and with rampant corruption sapping the empire's political vitality, the Barbarian tribes from northern and central Europe eventually overran imperial defenses. In 410 A.D., Rome was sacked by the Visigoths; the empire dissolved completely in 476, when a Germanic Barbarian king deposed the last Roman emperor. Had it not acquired land and begun to establish political control over what would become known as the Papal States, the church might also have fragmented more than it did and eventually disappeared. Instead, successive popes during the Dark and Middle Ages seized territory, waged war, negotiated treaties, and generally behaved much like the kings and princes who carved up Europe in general and Italy in particular. As the cities in Italy fortified themselves during the Middle Ages, so too did the Papal States.

The city of Rome lay within the borders of the Papal States and was governed by the pope. Thus, as the pope's fortunes rose and fell, so did those of the city. During the eleventh, twelfth, and thirteenth centuries, while the papacy was preoccupied with the Crusades—a series of military campaigns launched to recapture parts of Europe and the Holy Land from Muslim control—the city of Rome actually shrank. At the peak of the Roman Empire, Rome had boasted a population of 1.5 million people. Now a smaller and smaller population huddled in the shadows of the imperial ruins and clung to the filthy shores of the Tiber, contending with frequent floods and outbreaks of the plague. By the twelfth century, Rome was little more than a large village, with just 17,000 inhabitants.

Gone were the efficient sewage systems and functioning aqueducts of the Roman Empire. Drinking water was drawn primarily from the Tiber, the same

Piazzas, like Piazza Navona, have for centuries been an integral part of the Italian way of life, serving as living rooms, yards, markets, and parks.

river where waste was dumped—that is, if waste made it farther than the street outside the home. Most Romans lived in what today we might call tenements and row houses. Medieval Romans built relatively little compared to the Romans of the empire. Most of what they did build was constructed around piazzas, which, then as now, were noisy, social places lined with shops and markets and, in many cases, boasting fountains and public taps for the neighborhood.

A Church Divided

The pope, the spiritual and political leader of the Catholic Church, is elected from and by the College of Cardinals, a group of advisors, each of whom represents a different part of the Catholic world. By 1300, the appointment of cardinals had become a highly political process often involving the exchange of large sums of

money, political favors, and even murder. The cardinals and archbishops closest to Rome wielded the most power. Influential families and foreign governments jockeyed to install their favored candidates as cardinals, in the process creating a continually shifting network of power, corruption, and greed that dominated Rome's political life. Within the city, feudal families such as the Ferrara, the Este, the Rimini, the Colonna, and the Orsini vied with one another for supremacy in struggles that often turned bloody.

After much political maneuvering, the French wrested control of the College of Cardinals and succeeded in

The *Capitoline She-Wolf,* with twins Romulus and Remus suckling at her teats, is a ubiquitous symbol of ancient Rome. The statue was donated in 1471 by Pope Sixtus IV to the people of Rome and became one of the first items in the collection of the Musei Capitolini. The figure of the wolf dates to the fifth century B.C.; the twins were added some time in the sixteenth century. A replica of the famous bronze resides in the Campidoglio.

Romulus and Remus

Why is a she-wolf with two boys at her teats a symbol of Rome? According to legend, twin brothers Romulus and Remus were the sons of Mars, the god of war, and Rhea Silvia, a priestess. Rhea Silvia's father and uncle were locked in a bloody power struggle for their kingdom. Her uncle, Amulius, wanted his brother's bloodline to run dry, so he kidnapped the twin boys and set them adrift on a raft on the Tiber River. He never imagined the infants would survive.

The gods were watching, however, and they protected the boys, bringing their raft to shore far from Amulius's reach. There, a she-wolf found them. She suckled the boys and raised them until the three were discovered by a shepherd. He took the boys home, and they grew up in his care.

As young men, Romulus and Remus regained control of the kingdom their father had lost to his brother. But the younger brothers quarreled

over where to establish their new city. Romulus killed Remus and then established Rome on the Palatine Hill, the place where the she-wolf had found them.

Why Did Rome Become the Seat of Western Christianity?

The events of Jesus's life as presented in the New Testament all occurred in the Middle East, and Christianity began as a reformation movement within the Jewish community in ancient Israel. In the first century A.D., the Middle East was part of the Roman Empire. After Jesus's death, his disciples and missionaries spread across the empire and beyond. According to tradition, Jesus's disciples Peter and Paul both came to Rome.

Christian communities in Rome date to 40 A.D. and were tolerated, more or less. By 313, Christianity was a recognized religion in the empire. Emperor Constantine initiated an effort to codify and organize the religion in earnest. Constantine's efforts were not purely spiritual in nature, however. Doctrinal conflicts were occurring within Christian communities spread across the empire, threatening its stability. By imposing doctrinal conformity, Constantine was also imposing political unity in the far-flung empire.

Before his death, Jesus had said to Peter, "And I tell you that you are Peter, and on this rock I will build my church, and the gates of Hades will not overcome it. I will give you the keys of the kingdom of heaven; whatever you bind on earth will be bound in heaven, and whatever you loose on earth will be loosed in heaven." The papacy bases its earthly and spiritual authority on this passage. St. Peter, often depicted by painters and sculptors as holding two keys, is acknowledged as the first pope by Christians, though the title was bestowed posthumously.

As later Christians organized the church leadership, they looked to the Roman Empire for inspiration and divided the church geographically into dioceses, appointing bishops to oversee them. The bishop of Rome, who oversaw the most powerful diocese, became *primus inter pares* ("the first among equals"), and successive popes developed an elaborate administrative and canonical system to consolidate and wield their power. The system evolved as a patriarchy, with only men holding leadership

St. Peter is often portrayed with two keys in his hands. One represents the key to heaven, or his spiritual power; the other represents the key to earth, or temporal power. This statue is by Gian Lorenzo Bernini, the last architect to work on St. Peter's. Bernini designed the colonnade in Piazza San Pietro. Along the top of the colonnade sit 164 statues created by the sculptors in Bernini's workshop. All told, the figures took more than a century to complete.

positions. (The word "pope" comes from the Latin word *papa* and the Greek word *pappas*, both meaning "father.") Traditionally, all archbishops (administrators who oversee multiple dioceses) were assigned to a church in Rome regardless of where their dioceses were. This created strong ties to the city, even for far-flung archbishops.

For centuries, San Giovanni in Laterano—not the Vatican—has been the seat of the papacy in Rome. The first church on the site now occupied by San Giovanni in Laterano was a basilica built in the fourth century by Constantine. When the papacy moved to Avignon in the 1300s, the church and the papal palaces crumbled from neglect. After the pope's return to Rome, he moved across the river to San Pietro in Vaticano. The Vatican remains the papal residence, but San Giovanni in Laterano is still the official seat of the bishop of Rome and the City's Cathedral.

electing a French pope, who in 1305 whisked the papacy to Avignon, fearing for his life. The Italians refer to this period as the "Babylonian captivity," and bitterness about this event helps explains why very few non-Italian popes were elected. (After the death in 1523 of Adrian VI, a Dutchman, the church did not have another non-Italian pope for 455 years.) As the papacy went to Avignon, so too did money, the educated classes, and political power. Pope Gregory XI returned to Rome in 1377, but within a year the papacy again fell apart, descending into four decades of strife known as the Great Schism, during which two—and sometimes even three—popes claimed legitimacy at the same time. Without a leader, Romans were left to the mercy of brutal *condottieri* (mercenary leaders) and foreign kings who pillaged and plundered the city.

Order returned with the Council of Constance in 1417, which ended the dual papacies with the election of Martin V. When he came to Rome in 1420, Pope Martin "found it so dilapidated and deserted that it hardly bore any resemblance to a city." He recognized that the shabby city needed a physical manifestation of the papacy's claim to power. In other words, he needed to build.

In this painting from the fourteenth century, the Catholic Church is surrounded by heretics and unbelievers and defended by bishops, monks, and the pope. This depiction of a united church contrasts sharply with the bloody feuds and protracted schisms that characterized the papacy during the Middle Ages.

Martin V, a gifted administrator, began to reassert the control the popes had once exercised over all corners of the Papal States. In Rome itself, he not only began a program of restoration and new building but also ended a century of lawlessness. One man could not undo a hundred years' damage, however, and by the time of Martin's death in 1431, Rome was still far from being a synonym for grandeur.

The New Caesars, a New Rome

During the fifteenth century, commemorative medals were cast bearing the moniker *Roma caput mundi*—

The Colosseum dominated Rome until the new St. Peter's was built in the sixteenth century.

"Rome, the world's ruler." This claim was hardly accurate, but the men guiding the church and the city believed it to be destiny, and they saw a revival of Rome as a city of beauty and power as crucial to this goal.

The pontiffs of the fifteenth and sixteenth centuries also shared an ambition to recast the role of the papacy. Modeling themselves on the Caesars of the Roman Empire, the popes sought to present themselves as indomitable, magnificent rulers, their earthly grandeur reflecting their divine associations. Even in their personal lives, popes acted like kings and emperors, fathering illegitimate children, wrangling over money, feuding bitterly and bloodily, and enjoying lurid sexual adventures—all of which was fodder for delicious gossip, not for impassioned outrage, among the Roman public.

To impress their fellow Romans and visiting pilgrims with their imperial majesty, the popes embarked on a vast program of construction. Deteriorating churches bespoke papal weakness and decline, so all over Rome the churches of old were revisited and renovated as showcases of papal power. Meanwhile, in emulation of the Roman emperors who had built baths and civic parks to strengthen their support within the community, the popes began large civic building projects.

All these projects required building materials. Fortunately for papal ambitions, a ready supply was to be had right there in the heart of Rome: the ruins of the ancient empire.

The Renaissance popes did not intend to preserve the ruins. Indeed, they stripped them and destroyed many

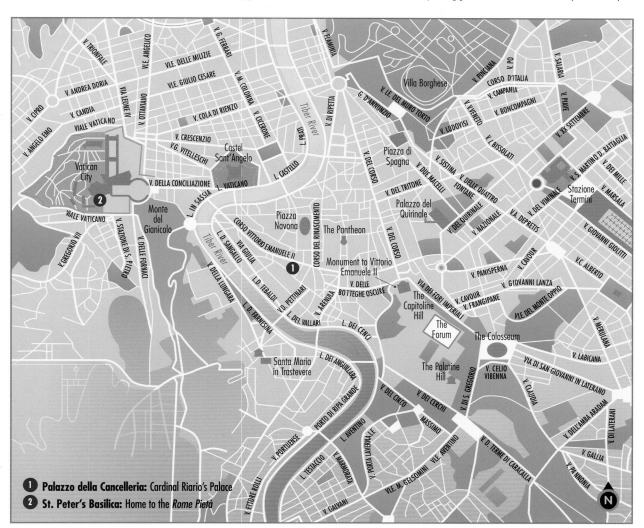

1 **Palazzo della Cancelleria:** Cardinal Riario's Palace
2 **St. Peter's Basilica:** Home to the *Rome Pietà*

entirely. But in the process, they inadvertently saved some ancient buildings by consecrating them as churches, and they preserved many fragments of other imperial architecture by reusing them in new structures. And they achieved their main goal: to make Rome spectacular.

Over the course of a century, the popes transformed Rome from a medieval village into a Renaissance jewel. They widened streets and constructed hospitals. They transformed entire neighborhoods, such as the Piazza Navona, which once had been a thriving marketplace. The papacy claimed the area for churches and palaces.

Although the popes took the lead in restoring Rome, they were not alone. Wealthy families from across Italy returned to Rome; by the early 1500s, the city boasted a population of more than 50,000 people. These families poured their fortunes into the city, competing among themselves to build ever larger and more opulent houses. Once its home was built, a family would often then devote its riches and energies to building and decorating churches, whose beauty advertised not only the glory of God but also the family's wealth and prestige.

Naturally enough in such an environment, artists found themselves in great demand—by the pope, by the cardinals, and by the upper classes. The demand was especially high as

the fifteenth century drew to a close, because Pope Alexander VI had decided to name 1500 a year of jubilee and had called for pilgrims to come to Rome. The church recognized that the pilgrims coming to Rome en masse would expect pageantry and grandeur—and if they found what they were looking for, they would spend money, a lot of money. The potential to fill the papal coffers was great, and Alexander VI was keen to maximize that potential by putting on a good show.

This map from 1493 shows a panoramic view of Rome from the Colosseum (on the left) to Castle Sant' Angelo (on the right).

Thus, when, on June 25, 1496, at the age of twenty-one, Michelangelo arrived in Rome, he found himself in exactly the right place at exactly the right time.

A New Home

Lorenzo de' Medici once called Rome "the receptacle of all the evils imaginable, with no shortage of inciters and corrupters." The city that greeted Michelangelo may have been in the process of beautification, but its political life was as ugly as ever. Cesare Borgia, son of Pope Alexander VI (1492–1503), employed thugs and

murderers to keep the city under his control. Prisons were full. Spies and assassins filled the streets. And Borgia extorted property from any aristocrat who dared to oppose him.

Having successfully navigated the misfortunes of the Medici, Michelangelo had learned to play the political games that would be necessary to win papal favor. He devoted himself to establishing his reputation during his first stay in Rome, which was to last nearly five years. This task would prove easier to accomplish than in Florence. In Rome, Michelangelo was out from under the shadow of the Florentine masters and closer to the heart of the Vatican—which had even more power and money than the Medici and the Borgia. In Florence, he had created half a dozen small sculptures, none of which had done much to bring him renown. In Rome, he set out to make a name for himself.

Michelangelo arrived bearing letters of introduction from Lorenzo di Pierfrancesco de' Medici that paved the way for him to present himself to Cardinal Raffaele Riario, the richest and most powerful cardinal in Rome. The cardinal offered Michelangelo a place to stay within his household. With 250 people in his retinue, the cardinal had the means to take on the young man. He was also a great collector of antiquities.

Palazzo della Cancellaria Apostolica
1. Chiesa di S. Lorenzo, e Damaso, 2. Vicolo de Leutari 3. Strada degli Argentieri, volgarmente detta del Pellegrino, 4. Palazzetto del Marchese Galli.

This engraving of the Palazzo della Cancelleria was made by Giuseppe Vasi in the mid-1700s. In addition to being Michelangelo's first home in Rome, for centuries the palazzo housed the papal government that ran the city.

Cardinal Riario, the cardinal of St. George, was in the middle of building a new palace, now known as the ❶ **Palazzo della Cancelleria**. Despite the ongoing construction, Michelangelo moved in. Sited in the middle of the Centro Storico—the historical center of the city—the Cancelleria gave Michelangelo easy access to the Pantheon, numerous churches, and the palazzi of the wealthiest Romans.

A week after he arrived, Michelangelo wrote to Lorenzo:

On Sunday the Cardinal came to the new house and asked for me; I went to him, and he asked me what I thought of the things I had seen. I told him what I felt about them, and certainly I felt that there were some very fine things. Then the

Popes during Michelangelo's Lifetime

1471–84: Sixtus IV (Family: della Rovere) rebuilt the Sistine Chapel as a fortress and decorated it with frescoes he received as a gift from Lorenzo de' Medici.

1484–92: Innocent VIII (Family: Cibò) played politics well. With strong ties to the Medici family, he built the Palazzo Belvedere at the Vatican. Originally a summer estate in the midst of meadows, the Palazzo Belvedere became the favored quarters for the popes and was eventually surrounded by the papal complex. It now houses some private rooms for the pope as well as part of the Vatican Museums.

1492–1503: Alexander VI (Family: Borgia), a ruthless pope, allowed his son, Cesare Borgia, to rule Rome with terror and cruelty.

1503: Pius III (Family: Piccolomini), may have been murdered to make way for his rival, Giuliano della Rovere.

1503–13: Julius II (Family: della Rovere) was Michelangelo's first papal patron. He commissioned his own tomb and began construction on the new St. Peter's Basilica. He also hired Michelangelo to fresco the ceiling of the Sistine Chapel.

1513–21: Leo X (Family: Medici) commissioned Michelangelo to create the façade of a small chapel inside Castel Sant'Angelo. He then sent Michelangelo back to Florence to work on the façade of San Lorenzo, the church where the Medici family worshipped.

1522–3: Adrian VI (Family: Boeyens) was the last non-Italian pope elected until Pope John Paul II in the twentieth century.

1523–34: Clement VII (Family: Medici) commissioned the Laurentian Library in Florence. Having escaped the Sack of Rome as a refugee, he eventually waded through a political morass and crowned Charles V, his one-time enemy, Holy Roman Emperor.

1534–9: Paul III (Family: Farnese) commissioned *The Last Judgment* as well as the Pauline Chapel and the Campidoglio. He also persuaded Michelangelo to take over the construction of St. Peter's Basilica and to finish the Palazzo Farnese.

1550–5: Julius III (Family: del Monte) and Michelangelo developed a close relationship and Julius III insisted that Michelangelo continue as architect of St. Peter's.

1555: Marcellus II (Family: Spannochi) was embarrassed by Michelangelo in front of Paul III when Marcellus was just a priest; the artist feared that as pope, Marcellus II would exact revenge. However, after only three weeks as pontiff, Marcellus II had a stroke and died.

1555–9: Paul IV (Family: Caraffa) considered destroying the Sistine Chapel and other "immodest" works of art.

1559–65: Pius IV (Family: Medici—the less-affluent Medici family in Milan) was Michelangelo's last patron. He commissioned the Sforza Chapel, the Porta Pia, and Santa Maria degli Angeli in an effort to leave his mark on Rome.

Cardinal asked me whether I was up to making something fine. I answered that I would not do such great things, but he would see what I would do. We have bought a piece of marble for a life-size figure, and I shall begin to work on Monday.

Surrounded by the "very fine things" of Rome, Michelangelo immediately set to work on his first large-scale piece.

Bacchus

Renaissance artists believed that works of art should be imitations of nature. Nature itself was regarded as both a creative phenomenon and something that could be observed and documented scientifically. Making a work of art required the same blend of creativity and science. Some artists, such as Albrecht Dürer, the German engraver who was a contemporary of Michelangelo, even tried to distill art down to mathematical proportions and formulas.

Bacchus (1497).

Anatomically Correct

Michelangelo approached the study of anatomy as a means of achieving greater beauty in his figures. He had studied dissection at Santo Spirito in Florence from 1492 to 1494. "He was very intimate with the prior, from whom he received much kindness and who provided him both with a room and with corpses for the study of anatomy, than which nothing could have given him greater pleasure." In his later years, though, Michelangelo had to give up dissection. Much to his chagrin, the stench of a decaying corpse made him ill.

The God of Wine

Bacchus, Michelangelo's first work created in Rome, depicts the Roman god of wine. Bacchus (known to the Greeks as Dionysus) taught humankind how to cultivate grapes and make wine, and was—appropriately enough—the god of merriment and revelry. The great dramas of the ancient world were performed in honor of Bacchus.

During the Renaissance, Romans drank wine at every meal. Like ale and beer in Europe's northern climes, wine in the south provided a safe, sterile drink that was far preferable to dirty river water. For a Roman, each day began with a small glass of wine, watered down slightly, and a piece of bread. People drank wine throughout the day as their primary beverage. Wine at breakfast may be out of fashion today, but *pane e vino* remains the foundation of the Roman diet.

Creating a lifelike image from flat plaster or solid marble certainly does require a solid understanding of mathematics, geometry, physics, and mechanics. In the quest for perfection, Renaissance artists fused art with science, seeking exact and accurate anatomy, proportions, scale, and perspective. Michelangelo mastered these rules and then learned to break them, taking sculpture beyond the achievements of the ancients. The artists of ancient Rome created lifelike forms from stone, but Michelangelo's fusion of precision and spirituality helped him to create figures that seem almost to breathe.

With *Bacchus* (which today can be found in Florence's Museo Nazionale del Bargello), Michelangelo learned to use the drill—a tool ancient Romans employed with great skill to create illusions that cannot be produced with chisels. While he tried out new techniques, Michelangelo also played with composition. Bacchus, as his blank gaze, unsteady posture, and precarious goblet of wine all attest, is drunk. The English poet Percy Bysshe Shelley later remarked that the figure "looks drunken, brutal, and narrow-minded, and has an expression of dissoluteness the most revolting."

Dirty Work

Marble comes from limestone and is of medium hardness. It is often chosen for sculpture because it can be polished to a high shine and because, through it, a sculptor can achieve remarkable levels of detail. But it is difficult to work with, as Leonardo da Vinci made clear:

> The sculptor in creating his work does so by the strength of his arm by which he consumes the marble, or other obdurate material in which his subject is enclosed: and this is done by most mechanical exercise, often accompanied by great sweat which mixes with the marble dust and forms a kind of mud daubed all over his face. The marble dust flours him all over so that he looks like a baker; his back is covered with a snowstorm of chips, and his house is made filthy by the flakes and dust of stone.

The contract between a patron and a sculptor usually stipulated the type of material to be used in a commissioned piece, the source of the material, the finish to be used, and the deadline for completion. A sculptor had to know his materials well when investing time and money in a block of stone. He had to consider the workability of the stone, its color, its durability, the size of the block needed, and how to transport it to his workshop, which was typically hundreds of miles from where the rock was quarried.

Sacred Sculpture

Sculpture as an art form went out of fashion with the rise of the early Christian church. The church founders considered the sculptures of the ancient Romans to be idols and demons, and the sculpting of freestanding forms eventually became taboo. Yet, human and animal figures persisted in church and domestic decoration in the form of relief and architectural elements. When, around 1440, the Florentine sculptor Donatello unveiled his *David*, a new artistic era began.

Donatello's bronze was not only the first freestanding figure of the Renaissance but also a nude. Emboldened by his example, sculptors began to imitate classical figures that could still be found throughout Italy.

For Michelangelo, the ideal sculpture emerged from a single block of marble, which meant he had to be especially careful in choosing his stone. Like many sculptors, he often visited the quarries in Pietrasanta and Carrara in Tuscany, where marble has been quarried since the first century A.D. To make sure he could get the finest stone, Michelangelo cultivated close relationships with quarry workers, compensating them generously. In return, they labored loyally and diligently on his behalf in a perilous line of work. The sculptor himself was nearly killed one day in a quarry when a ring supporting the ropes around a large block of marble snapped, sending the rock hurtling downhill toward him.

To quarry marble, Renaissance workers inserted a series of wooden wedges into cracks in the stone. When they poured water over the wedges, the wedges swelled. The process was repeated over and over again until the block split away from the mountain. The stones were then given a "rough dressing"—shaped into usable blocks—before being shipped away.

The tools of a sculptor have hardly changed since Michelangelo's day.

A Sonnet by Michelangelo (undated)

If my rough hammer in hard stones can form
A human semblance, one and then another,
Set moving by the agent who is holder,
Watcher and guide, its course is not its own.

But that divine One, staying in Heaven at home,
Gives others beauty, more to itself, self-mover;
If hammers can't be made without a hammer,
From that one living all the others come.

And since a blow will have the greatest force
As at the forge it's lifted up the highest,
This above mine to Heaven has run and flown.

Wherefore with me, unfinished, all is lost.
Unless the divine workshop will assist
In making it; on earth it was alone.

Once stone arrived in his workshop, Michelangelo used large chisels and drills to remove the bulk of the stone, gradually transitioning to finer chisels for the detailed work. He used both small and full-sized models based on his sketches to guide his work. Made from clay, the models were supported by a wooden armature. If the figure was to be clothed, the model could be draped in cloth dipped in clay to give it beautiful, flowing, but permanent folds of voluminous cloth.

Michelangelo worked on full-scale figures in the same way that he did relief: from the front to the back. He would make a wax model of the figure and lay it in a pan of water. Then, as he worked back through the marble, he raised more and more of it from the water, revealing the figure a bit at a time.

He did not "finish" every inch of his pieces; rather, he left parts of each sculpture in rough rock, a testament to their origins and to his love of stone in its raw form. The proportions of the original marble block can be gauged from the size of the base of each piece. The finishing process—and the sculpting process itself—was dirty and dangerous, much like quarrying. As he hammered against his chisels, metal on metal against stone, chips flew. He did not wear safety glasses. The hammers and chisels and stones were heavy and bulky and sharp. Sculpting was bruising, sweaty work—but it was also inspiring for Michelangelo, who not only wrote poems about sculpting but also while sculpting.

To light his workshop, Michelangelo spent money on expensive candles made of pure goat's tallow. He often worked into the night, carving and polishing in the candles' golden glow. He constructed a "helmet made of pasteboard holding a burning candle over the middle of his head which shed light where he was working without tying up his hands," a biographer noted. Michelangelo used light—both natural and candlelight—to guide him as he created different textures: cloth, skin, hair, wood—each with its own sheen and depth. He often worked on several pieces at once. He carved constantly, taking pleasure and solace in his work.

The *Rome Pietà*

Cardinal Riario may have invited Michelangelo to join his entourage, but he did not like what Michelangelo produced from that first block of marble. So the young man found another buyer for *Bacchus*, Jacopo Galli, a wealthy collector of antiquities. Galli then worked on Michelangelo's behalf to help him find his next commission. It came from a powerful French cardinal, Jean Bilhères, who wanted Michelangelo to create a grave marker for himself to be placed in St. Peter's Basilica. The contract, signed by Galli

The *Rome Pietà* (1499). A pietà is a traditional Christian composition featuring Mary mourning over the crucified body of her son. Michelangelo carved three pietàs during his lifetime. His first is known as the *Rome Pietà* because of its location. The other two are the *Rondanini Pietà*, which can be found in Milan's Castello Sforzesco, and the *Florentine Pietà*, which is in the Museo dell'Opera del Duomo in Florence.

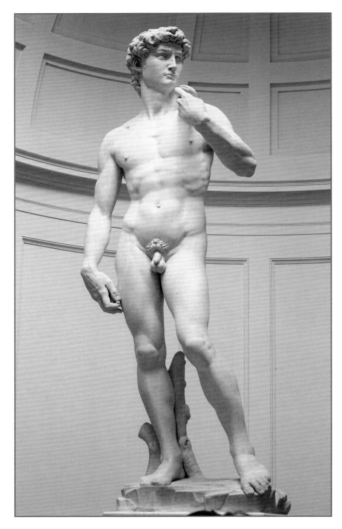

Michelangelo's *David* (1504) is known by Florentines as *Il Gigante,* the giant. Moving it from his workshop to its first public location in the Piazza della Signoria took several days. In its original spot, *David* stood guarding the entrance to the seat of Florence's government as a symbol of civic pride and virtue. In 1874, the sculpture was moved to the Galleria dell'Accademia; a replica remains in the Piazza della Signoria.

and Michelangelo, read: "I Jacopo Galli promise the Reverend Monsignor that the said Michelangelo will do the said work in a year and it will be the most beautiful marble which can be seen in Rome today, and that no other master could make it better today."

Michelangelo traveled to Carrara to choose a large piece of high-quality marble for the work. The contract called for a sculpture of Mary holding the crucified Jesus. The composition Michelangelo created involved carving two full-sized figures from one block of marble—a difficult task. Michelangelo bent the rules of proportion to his own purposes: Mary is much larger than Jesus to support the weight of a life-sized figure in her lap, but their heads are the same size, making the difference in size hard to detect. Mary's size serves a structural purpose, but it also allows the grieving mother to hold her son on her lap, creating a tableau that is both powerful and tender.

The *Rome Pietà*—as it is now known—was installed in St. Peter's and was immediately acclaimed as a work of supreme beauty and skill. But as he stood in the basilica one day, Michelangelo overheard someone attribute the piece to Gobbo, a sculptor from Milan. Michelangelo grabbed his tools and returned to add one final touch to the piece: his signature on the sash across Mary's chest. It was the only piece he ever signed.

Today the *Rome Pietà* occupies a side chapel in
❷ **St. Peter's Basilica,** separated from viewers by thick panes of bulletproof glass installed after a vandal attacked the piece with a hammer in 1972. Before St. Peter's was rebuilt, the sculpture sat on the floor above a tomb. Today it is displayed on a pedestal in a secluded chapel, which prevents it from being seen at its best angle. Some experts believe

that if it were moved to a dark church, the lighting would shift the focus away from Mary and on to Christ.

Michelangelo's *Rome Pietà* was recognized as extraordinary for its emotional depth, as well as for its technical mastery, and the artist's reputation rapidly grew. He had achieved his goal: in his five years in Rome, he had established himself as a sculptor in demand.

SPQR

The empire may have dissolved after Rome was sacked by the Visigoths in 410 A.D., but the spirit of the empire never died. Modern Rome bears the stamp of ancient Rome in places both pedestrian and noble. Everywhere, from lampposts and trashcans to pope's tombs and T-shirts, the letters SPQR invoke the spirit in which the city was founded: *Senatus Populusque Romanus*, meaning "the Senate and the people of Rome."

When reports of Michelangelo's success reached Florence, his father was both pleased and upset: pleased because his son was evidently on the threshold of a lucrative career, upset because as long as his son remained in Rome, he, the father, would have a difficult time grabbing a slice of his son's wealth. He wrote to Michelangelo, pressing him for money and urging him to return to Florence. Answering his father's call, Michelangelo left Rome—but only for a short time.

Return to Florence

Politically, Florence was calmer than when Michelangelo had left. Savonarola had met his fate: hanged publicly, his corpse was burned like so many of the artworks he had destroyed. The French controlled the city, having been allowed to enter by Piero de' Medici in 1494, but relative peace had returned, allowing the inhabitants to get back to work and the wealthy to hire artists again.

Michelangelo returned to Florence a successful artist, and soon received well-paid commissions from a range of patrons, some quite powerful, in his native city. One commission would further enhance and forever cement his reputation as a great sculptor: *David*. The block of marble from which *David* was carved had been quarried nearly half a century before. Two other artists had attempted to work with it but had found it too huge and flawed. The block had lain abandoned for years.

Nearly seventeen feet tall, Michelangelo's sculpture portrays the biblical King David as a powerful, muscular young man gazing intently at his unseen target, Goliath, just before loading his slingshot. His physique and stance suggest an ancient Apollo—godlike and idealized. Completed and installed in 1504, the piece made Michelangelo famous throughout Italy.

The achievement brought him to the attention of the new pope, Julius II, who had been elected by the cardinals in 1503. Julius wanted an elaborate tomb for himself, and he decided to entrust the task to Italy's new star. Michelangelo eagerly accepted the commission and promptly returned to Rome to start work. However, Julius's tomb would take far longer to complete than anyone could have imagined.

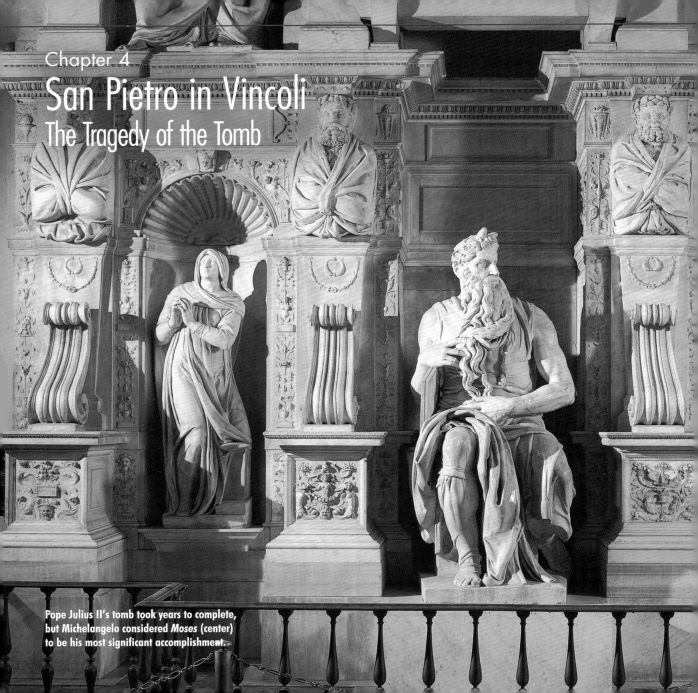

Chapter 4

San Pietro in Vincoli
The Tragedy of the Tomb

Pope Julius II's tomb took years to complete, but Michelangelo considered *Moses* (center) to be his most significant accomplishment.

With the papal summons to Rome, young Michelangelo was officially being celebrated across the peninsula as a genius. The *Rome Pietà* had cemented his reputation in Rome. *David* had established him as a great artist in Florence. And now the pope wanted his services. Michelangelo had finally arrived: he had secured a patron with power, influence, and deep pockets.

An impatient man, Michelangelo was frustrated that the pope did not summon him for an audience as soon as he arrived in Rome. But Julius II was carefully considering how to use the artist. Michelangelo waited many months in Rome before the pope decided on his commission. In April 1505, Michelangelo and the pope signed a contract for 10,000 ducats in exchange for a monumental tomb for the pope.

Julius II's tomb was to be enormous, enough work for a lifetime. The tomb reflected the ambition and arrogance of both the pope and the sculptor—traits that bonded the two but that also set them at odds.

The tomb was originally to be installed in San Pietro in Vincoli, the church where Julius II had served before becoming pope. But as the plans expanded, the pope had a better idea for the tomb's placement: St. Peter's Basilica. When Michelangelo surveyed

St. Peter's, though, he determined that the tomb that he had designed would not fit. Rather than scale back his ambitions, he suggested that the church be expanded. Julius II agreed and ordered designs for a renovated St. Peter's to be prepared. Michelangelo was given an advance of one hundred gold florins, the equivalent of a year's pay, and the pope's blessing to travel to Carrara to choose the marble for the tomb. Michelangelo left almost immediately, spending eight months selecting stone with which to begin the project.

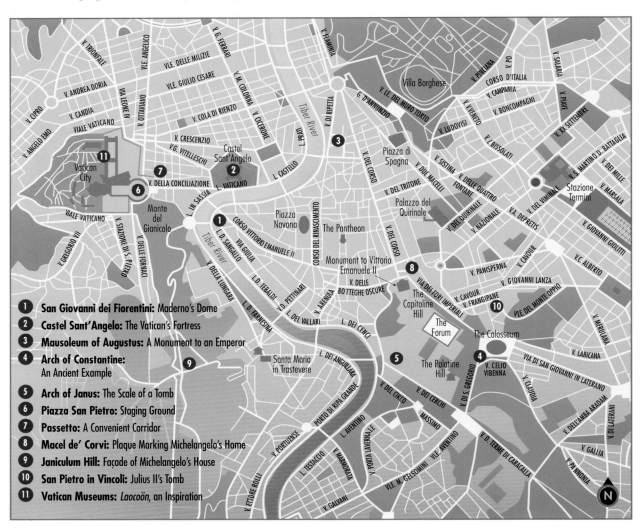

1. **San Giovanni dei Fiorentini:** Maderno's Dome
2. **Castel Sant'Angelo:** The Vatican's Fortress
3. **Mausoleum of Augustus:** A Monument to an Emperor
4. **Arch of Constantine:** An Ancient Example
5. **Arch of Janus:** The Scale of a Tomb
6. **Piazza San Pietro:** Staging Ground
7. **Passetto:** A Convenient Corridor
8. **Macel de' Corvi:** Plaque Marking Michelangelo's Home
9. **Janiculum Hill:** Façade of Michelangelo's House
10. **San Pietro in Vincoli:** Julius II's Tomb
11. **Vatican Museums:** *Laocoön*, an Inspiration

Feared, Hated, and Respected

In Julius II, pope from 1503 to 1513, Michelangelo found an influential friend and a frustrating adversary. The most powerful of the Renaissance popes, Julius II came from the wealthy della Rovere family. In 1503, he was a youthful sixty-year-old man with energy, ideas, and enthusiasm. He hated the French, loved war, and wanted to establish the papacy as a powerful force independent of the Roman families who tried to interfere in papal politics. Some feared him, others hated him, and all respected him.

By the time he summoned Michelangelo, the ambitious pope had lived in the Eternal

Michelangelo and Julius II in a painting by Anastagio Fontebuori.

City since 1471 and despaired over its state of decay. Cows grazed in the buildings and temples of the Forum. Peasants tended their vineyards on the Palatine Hill, wandering through palatial remains. The Circus Maximus hosted gardeners tending their plots rather than drawing crowds for chariot races. Raw sewage stank in the streets, and the Tiber reeked with refuse. The city known as the world's capital looked and smelled like the remains of an ancient festival long forgotten.

With full coffers and political savvy, Julius II aimed to continue Pope Martin V's work in turning the dirty,

Lined with shops and restaurants, fashionable Via Giulia lies in the center of the bustling city. To build it, Julius II demolished existing homes and shops, hoping to create a city of straight, wide boulevards.

run-down city into a beacon of Christianity, but he had larger diplomatic goals, too. He wanted to regain the church's autonomy and to get out from under the influence of foreign kings and emperors. His war cry became, "Out with the barbarians!" He recognized Rome's importance as the center of a faded empire and its potential to become a gleaming symbol of a reinvigorated Catholic Church—a capital to rival London or Paris.

Julius decided to begin with the papal palace and the behemoth St. Peter's, but his program of improvement grew during his ten years as pope to include bridges, villas, piazzas, and, ultimately, a historic redesign of the city complete with boulevards and civic monuments. To get a feel for Julius II's vision of Rome, a visitor might walk Via Giulia, the straightest street in the city. Julius II demolished countless buildings to make way for a wide, straight path from the Ponte Principe Amedeo along the river. Here, charming buildings line a street largely unchanged since the sixteenth century. Among those buildings is the ❶ church of San Giovanni dei Fiorentini, which sports a dome designed by Carlo Maderno, who was influenced by Michelangelo's dome for St. Peter's Basilica. Pets are welcome at the church, and well-behaved cats and dogs often attend services.

Monumental Influences

Great cities celebrate their great leaders, and as the self-appointed director of Rome's rebirth, Julius II wanted to celebrate himself. Born Giuliano della Rovere, he chose as his papal name the name of one of Rome's great emperors, and he wanted to be memorialized in the grandest Roman style. Thus, he chose the finest sculptor in Italy to construct what was to be the largest tomb in Rome since the days of the Empire.

Roman emperors, like the popes after them, often began building their tombs as soon as they came to power. The tombs represented power, greatness, and eternity. They dot the city of Rome today—some still standing as tombs, others requisitioned for different purposes. As Julius II looked to the past for a precedent, he had only to look out his window: ❷ **Castel Sant'Angelo** began as Hadrian's Mausoleum.

Gregory the Great renamed Hadrian's Mausoleum Castel Sant'Angelo in the sixth century. Rome was suffering from the plague, and Pope Gregory had a vision of St. Michael on the mausoleum, which he interpreted to mean that the plague was over. Eventually, the Vatican converted Castel Sant'Angelo from a mausoleum into a fortress, and then into a castle connected to the papal quarters via a fortified passageway.

Built during the second century A.D., Hadrian's Mausoleum was used as the emperors' burial place for almost a century. The structure was originally covered in marble and travertine, topped with a mound of earth planted with trees, surrounded by statues, and crowned with a statue of Hadrian and a four-horse chariot.

In the Middle Ages, the mausoleum was transformed into a fortress and altered significantly to become the Vatican's stronghold, prison, and, for a time, treasury. The statue of Hadrian, removed long ago, was replaced by an angel, hence the name Castel Sant'Angelo. Now a museum, Castel Sant'Angelo offers a delightful view of the city as well as a café at the top of the structure.

To access the mausoleum from the city center, Hadrian built the Aelian Bridge, now known as the Ponte Sant'Angelo, across the Tiber. Today the Ponte

Sant'Angelo features figures of angels designed by Gian Lorenzo Bernini (1598–1680).

Hadrian was not the first to build a monumental burial ground. Up the river from Hadrian's Mausoleum lies the ❸ **Mausoleum of Augustus.** Augustus began his mausoleum in 29 B.C. after seeing Alexander the Great's tomb in Alexandria, Egypt. Although it has now been stripped of much of its grandeur, it was an imposing monument in its time. It, too, was topped with trees and two levels of garden areas. Two obelisks flanked the doors; both were removed during the

A Leonine Façade

Pope Leo X (pope from 1513 to 1521), the successor to Pope Julius II and a Medici, was eager to put Michelangelo to work for him as well, but he allowed the artist to return to Florence to work for the Medici there. Before he left Rome in 1515, though, Michelangelo designed the façade for a small chapel in the Castel Sant'Angelo. The façade anchors a wall with a graceful and elegant simplicity, beautifying an otherwise unremarkable courtyard. The lion heads are a play on Leo's name; his symbols—a ring and feathers—cap the composition, incorporating the papal signature. The marble for the project probably came from the stores procured for Julius II's tomb.

Below the chapel lie dungeons, reminders that Castel Sant'Angelo served as Rome's prison during the fifteenth and sixteenth centuries.

Like other grandiose mausoleums in ancient Rome, the Mausoleum of Augustus was not only a monument to the dead but a gathering place for the living. Today, only parts of the original building remain. Augustus (27 B.C.–14 A.D.) and his family were buried here; over the centuries, it was used for a variety of purposes including as a fortress.

building craze of the Renaissance. Romans have used the Mausoleum of Augustus in a variety of ways, including as a venue for public gatherings and shows. During Mussolini's reign, excavations cleared away additions made over the centuries to reveal what remains of the original structure.

The original design for Julius II's tomb incorporated ideas from not only the imperial mausoleums but also the triumphal arches of imperial Rome. The ancient Romans marked events of historic significance—often victory in battle—by erecting imposing arches. Public monuments extolling virtue and valor, the arches celebrated the might of the Roman Empire.

Julius II and Michelangelo probably looked to the ❹ **Arch of Constantine** as a model. Erected as part of a celebration of the tenth year of the emperor's reign (315 A.D.), the arch commemorates Constantine's military and civic accomplishments. Its creators poached reliefs from other Roman edifices to complete it quickly.

When Michelangelo walked to the Arch of Constantine, however, he wouldn't have been able to see it in its entirety. The city had engulfed the monument, burying more than half of it under dirt and debris and surrounding it with homes and businesses. The arch, like Augustus's Mausoleum, was not completely excavated until the twentieth century.

Both the pope and the sculptor almost certainly devoted a lot of attention to the ❺ **Arch of Janus,** which in size and scale closely resembles the monument Julius planned for himself. Located steps away from the church of Santa Maria in Cosmedin and its famous marble disk called the Mouth of Truth

The Arch of Constantine.

(an ancient drain cover that, according to legend, bites the hand of a liar), the Arch of Janus was erected in 357 A.D. to celebrate the Roman god of beginnings and endings.

Although the original design for Julius II's tomb does not survive, documents from the time indicate that the freestanding structure was to measure twenty-three feet long by thirty-six feet wide and was to be as high as it was long: roughly the size of the Arch of Janus. It was to be dominated by four main figures and topped with a larger-than-life-size sculpture of Julius II himself.

The tomb was intended to portray Julius II as a patron of learning and the liberal arts. More than forty carved figures were to anthropomorphize the fine arts, including grammar, rhetoric, arithmetic, logic, music, astronomy, geometry, painting, sculpture, and architecture. In addition, angels were to flit about the structure, and bronze reliefs were to illustrate scenes from Julius II's life.

The Arch of Janus.

Conflict

Michelangelo returned to Rome from Carrara in the winter of 1506. Before he left the city the previous spring, he secured a studio where he could live and work. His house stood on Piazza Rusticucci, a humble, quiet piazza with a simple little church, Santa Caterina delle Cavallerotte. The studio, the piazza, and the church are no longer there; tourist shops and Vatican offices now dominate the area, which lies between Piazza San Pietro and Via della Conciliazione.

Michelangelo, who had stopped to visit his family in Florence on his way home, found when he arrived in Rome that the marble had preceded him and was waiting at the port. He had the blocks transported to the ❻ **Piazza San Pietro.** The Italian piazza, like the town square in the United States or the *place* in France, is where society gathers. To place marble in the piazza, then, was to invite inspection, conversation, and admiration.

In the meantime, the pope had decided he needed better access to Michelangelo's studio; fortunately, he found an easy solution. Centuries earlier, a fortified passageway had been built between the Vatican and Castel Sant'Angelo to enable popes to be whisked away when in danger. From the ❼ **Passetto** (which means "corridor"), Julius II built a drawbridge to Michelangelo's studio. This way he could secretly visit Michelangelo without having to walk across the public piazza. Among its other advantages, such a discreet route meant that other artists, such as Bramante, would not be aware—and thus would not be jealous—of the time and attention Julius II lavished on the sculptor.

Purchasing the mountain of marble—more than ninety wagonloads—from Carrara and moving it to Rome cost a great sum. Michelangelo paid for the expenses from his own coffers. Julius II had insisted that Michelangelo come to him personally in matters of finance, so a few days after settling into his house on Piazza Rusticucci, Michelangelo walked the short distance to the papal palace to collect on his expenses.

Michelangelo explained in a letter to his friend Giuliano da Sangallo what happened next:

Christian Burials in Ancient Rome

During the first and second centuries A.D., the bodies of Roman emperors and common citizens were typically cremated. The law forbade cremation and burials within city walls, so crematoriums were built outside the city. Some Romans, however, buried their dead. Wealthy families often owned mausoleums where they buried their ancestors in sarcophagi or placed their ashes in urns. On holidays and during certain celebrations, families ventured out to their mausoleums to make offerings of wine, olive oil, and bread to their ancestors.

Christians were especially likely to opt for burial—and for a very practical reason: they believed in an imminent resurrection, for which they would need their bodies. Bodies of those not wealthy enough to have a mausoleum were buried in catacombs. The soil in many places in Rome is such that when exposed to air, it hardens into stone, which is perfect for carving out tunnels lined with burial chambers. Families were required to purchase clay seals for each tomb—signed and dated indications that the burial taxes had been paid.

Modern misconceptions hold that Christians chose the catacombs as places to bury their dead out of fear of persecution. Although persecution was certainly a reality, the catacombs were sanctioned—indeed, taxable—places for burial. Christian churches and gathering places did, however, crop up around the catacombs, because the burial grounds held the remains of saints.

On Holy Saturday I heard the Pope, speaking at table with a jeweler and the Master of Ceremonies, say that he didn't want to spend a penny more either on large or small stones, which amazed me a good deal. Still before I left I asked him for part of what I needed for going on with the work. His Holiness answered me that I should come back Monday; and I came back there Monday and Tuesday and Wednesday and Thursday, as he saw.

When he returned on Saturday, the doorman refused him entry:

"Forgive me, but I have orders not to admit you." There was a bishop present, who when he overheard the equerry's words rebuked him, saying, "You must not realize who this man is?" "On the contrary, I do know him," answered the equerry, "but I am obliged to follow the orders of my superiors, without inquiring further."

Barred from Julius II's presence and denied the money he was owed, Michelangelo replied, "And you may tell the

pope that from now on, if he wants me, he can look for me elsewhere." Michelangelo returned to his studio. His pride injured, and tired of papal politics, he and his servants sold all his furniture, packed their belongings, and set out for Florence in April 1506.

Despite his reluctance to pay Michelangelo, Julius II did not want to stall progress on his tomb. He sent five couriers to follow Michelangelo and his retinue; they caught up to the travelers outside of Rome. The letter the couriers bore commanded Michelangelo to return

This undated sketch by Michelangelo shows part of an early design for Julius II's tomb. It is interesting to note that the actions and poses of the angels and cherubs in this sketch are mirrored in the nudes in the Sistine Chapel ceiling.

to Rome at once. Michelangelo replied that "he would never go back; that in return for his good and faithful service he did not deserve to be driven from the pope's presence like a villain; and that, since His Holiness no longer wished to pursue the tomb, he was freed from his obligation and did not wish to commit himself to anything else."

Sending the couriers on their way, Michelangelo hurried to Florence. The couriers knew that they faced the wrath of the pope if they returned without Michelangelo. The sculptor had offered to lie to the pope, saying they had found him in Florence, beyond papal jurisdiction.

Julius II's refusal to pay Michelangelo reflected a change in papal finances and priorities. While Michelangelo had been in Carrara, Julius II's focus had shifted. As Michelangelo had recommended, the pope had commissioned designs to rebuild St. Peter's to accommodate his tomb, and a design by Bramante had been chosen. But the new plan called for an enormous building that would require commensurate funding. Julius II saw this as an opportunity to build not just a monumental tomb but also a monumental church as part of his legacy in Rome—but he needed funds to make his vision a reality. The Papal States were an obvious source of funding for projects through taxes and trade, but papal control over those territories had weakened during the previous century. Thus, the pope set off with an army of mercenaries to bring the Papal States back in line and refill the depleted coffers.

Macel de' Corvi

Michelangelo's house at ❽ **Macel de' Corvi** sat across from the church of Santa Maria di Loreto. The artist lived here on and off after Julius II's death in 1513. The house proved to be a point of contention in the forty-year struggle between Michelangelo and Julius II's heirs to complete the tomb. A simple but ample dwelling, it boasted high ceilings, a garden, and a grand staircase. Over the staircase, Michelangelo painted a skeleton with a coffin—perhaps an example of his dark sense of humor.

After his death, the house remained standing until 1875, when it was demolished along with many other buildings in the area to make way for the Monument to Vittorio Emanuele II (1820–78), the last king of Piedmont-Sardinia and the first king of the united Italy. The façade was saved, however, and in 1941 it was moved to the ❾ **Janiculum Hill** and installed on the front of a building housing a water reservoir.

Macel de' Corvi was part of Michelangelo's compensation for Julius II's tomb. Macel de' Corvi, or Slaughterhouse of the Crows, is actually the name of the neighborhood where the original house stood. The façade of Michelangleo's house is now on the Janiculum Hill.

While the pope was off making war, however, he did not forget about Michelangelo, who had settled down in Florence. Letters from Julius II demanding Michelangelo's presence in Rome arrived regularly. Piero Soderini, the *gonfaloniere* of Florence, finally intervened. Fearing that Julius II would bring his military campaign to Florence in pursuit of the artist, Soderini sent Michelangelo to Bologna, where Julius II had just declared victory.

San Pietro in Vincoli, home to Julius II's tomb, is an unimposing but charming basilica that is rarely crowded even though it is home to what Michelangelo considered his greatest sculpture.

"No sooner had [Michelangelo] pulled off his boots," recorded Vasari,

> than he was brought by the pope's servants before His Holiness. When they came before the pope and Michelangelo knelt down, His Holiness looked at him askance and, as if he were angry, he said, "Rather than coming to meet Us, you have waited for Us to come to meet you?" meaning to infer that Bologna was closer to Florence than to Rome. With courteous gestures and a loud voice, Michelangelo humbly begged the pope's pardon, excusing himself, since he had acted in anger, having been unable to bear being chased away in such a fashion, and he begged the pope once again to forgive him for having done wrong.

A bishop in attendance tried to help Michelangelo's cause, "declaring to His Holiness that such men were ignorant and worthless in anything outside of their art." Julius II flew into a rage, beating the bishop with his mace and screaming, "You are the ignorant one, speaking insults We would never utter!"

With that, Michelangelo and Julius II settled into a peaceful patronage. The pope commissioned a bronze statue of himself to be placed above the door of San Petronio in Bologna. Michelangelo set to work on the statue. In preliminary models, he depicted Julius holding a book in his hand. The pope scoffed, "I know nothing about literature!" Michelangelo put a sword in his hand instead. A few years later, the bronze of Julius was melted down by the people of Bologna in an act of defiant revenge. Not even a sketch of it survives.

Changing Times

Tombs exist to keep the dead alive in the memories of the living. When Julius II died in 1513, the plans for his tomb were immediately scaled back. The original plan would have consumed a sizable fortune, with which his heirs were not willing to part. And the election of Leo X after Julius II's death ensured that the tomb project would not continue according to the original plan, for Leo X hailed from the Medici family and would not allow a della Rovere pope's tomb to dominate the St. Peter's structure now under his control.

For more than thirty years, Julius II's tomb haunted Michelangelo. It became a political pawn for powerful families and a personal crusade for the artist, who at times found his reputation impugned by the other players in the drama. In 1542, Michelangelo wrote to a member of the College of Cardinals, "I say and affirm that either for damages or interest five thousand ducats is due me from the heirs of Pope Julius; and in the meantime those who have taken all

Laocoön

In January 1506, word spread of a tremendous sculpture discovered in a vineyard near Santa Maria Maggiore. Julius II sent a servant and Michelangelo to see what was happening, and so it was that Michelangelo witnessed the excavation of the most famous discovery of his day: *Laocoön*, exhumed from the Sette Sale of the Domus Aurea.

According to legend, Laocoön, a priest, angered the gods. During the Trojan war, he warned his fellow Trojans of the danger in accepting the wooden horse from the Greeks, but to no avail. At the behest of the gods, snakes came from the sea, snatched Laocoön and his sons, and dragged them to a watery death.

Depicting Laocoön and his two sons in mortal struggle with writhing serpents, *Laocoön* had been buried for centuries. Julius II bought the sculpture and placed it in the Belvedere Courtyard for artists to study and admire. As Michelangelo planned Pope Julius II's tomb, he undoubtedly drew inspiration from the muscled angst of the ancient sculpture. *Laocoön* now resides in the ⑪ **Vatican Museums.**

Laocoön.

my youth and honor and property from me call me a thief!" That same year, Michelangelo entered into the last contract for the tomb. This final contract stipulated not only a much less ambitious design but also a less prominent location—not in St. Peter's but in ❿ **San Pietro in Vincoli.** This modest basilica north of the Colosseum had been Julius II's cardinal seat. Called "St. Peter in Chains," the church houses two sets of chains. Reputedly, these chains held Peter while he was in jail in Jerusalem and when he was imprisoned in Rome. The two are said to have fused together miraculously; they can now be seen in the confessional beneath the high altar.

In Bondage to This Tomb

Although Julius II's tomb is remarkable, Michelangelo described the finished work as "the tragedy of the tomb": "I find I have lost all my youth bound to this tomb," he wrote.

For decades, Michelangelo had worked on figures for Julius II's tomb, often in secret so that his other patrons would not know of his divided attention. The figure he completed first was *Moses*. A cardinal who had come to Michelangelo's studio to see another project said upon seeing

According to legend, Michelangelo found *Moses* to be so lifelike that he once struck the sculpture's knee and called out, "Speak, damn you!"

Leah.

Slaves

Originally destined for Julius II's tomb, six slave figures, two of which were made in Rome and four in Florence, show Michelangelo's mastery of expressive form and vividly display his carving techniques. Their contrasting poses offer an impressive range of expression, from the languid *Dying Slave* to the taut *Block-Head Slave.*

Some scholars contend that the slaves (or "captives," as they are also known) are unfinished works, with much of the stone still rough and unpolished or shaped. Whether Michelangelo would have agreed with these scholars is questionable. The fragments and ruins of imperial Rome fueled his imagination precisely because they were incomplete. In Michelangelo's mind, the unfinished conveyed the essence of and the idea behind a piece. His goal was not an exact replica; rather, he aimed to create a moment, an idea, releasing the figure "hidden" inside the stone. As he wrote in a sonnet addressed to his friend Vittoria Colonna:

> *No block of marble but it does not hide*
> *the concept living in the artists' mind_*
> *pursuing it inside that form, he'll guide*
> *his hand to shape what reason had defined.*

Moses, "This statue alone is sufficient to do honor to the tomb of Pope Julius."

Moses illustrates Michelangelo's brilliance as a sculptor. At the moment depicted, Moses has just descended from Mount Sinai, having seen God and been given the law on the stone tablets under his arm. The Old Testament describes him as glowing in the "radiance of the Lord," but a medieval translator mistakenly rendered the phrase as having horns, so Michelangelo presents Moses with satyr's horns protruding from his forehead. The figure's torso is disproportionately long (he would be ten feet tall if he stood up) to give him power and presence; this trick is concealed from the viewer by Moses's muscular arms and flowing beard.

Moses dominates the tomb, but it is flanked by two other figures, *Leah* and *Rachel*, which represent, respectively, the active and the contemplative life and introduce theological ideas hotly debated during the Reformation. Rachel represents faith, whereas her sister Leah embodies charity. In these two figures, Michelangelo refers to the debate raging over salvation through faith as opposed to salvation through works—a topic he often discussed with friends in his later years.

In depicting Moses, Leah, and Rachel on Julius II's tomb, Michelangelo is comparing the pope to the man who released the Israelites from captivity and talked with God. The illustration would have been even more complete with the inclusion of the slave figures Michelangelo had been working on, but these figures were cast aside at some point in the decades of redesign.

In the end, only one face of the original four-faced design was installed, and it too was scaled back. Michelangelo's assistants built the structure and sculpted the other figures, including the reclining figure of Julius II, Mary holding baby Jesus, the sibyl, the prophet, and four men in relief. The marble, quarried at different times and from different sources, does not all match. And Julius II's remains were never removed from his "temporary" grave in St. Peter's.

Julius II left the papacy stronger, wealthier, and larger. His personality and charisma allowed him great liberties and generated both respect and fear. Michelangelo found Julius II to be a kindred spirit, but theirs was a tumultuous relationship, one of battles and tantrums. The sculptor wrote of the pope, "One who knows how to handle him and who has given him trust, always will find him the best disposed person in the world."

Julius II had wanted Michelangelo to build him a tomb that would impress history with its opulence and

Rachel.

majesty. In the end, however, the pope's tomb, for all the sculptor's skill, is underwhelming. Yet, Julius can hardly be considered a minor figure in Michelangelo's story. Not only was he one of Michelangelo's greatest patrons, friends, and enemies, but he also set Michelangelo to work on what would become the artist's most famous project: the Sistine Chapel.

After only a few decades, however, the chapel's roof had begun to leak and structural repairs were needed. When Pope Julius II was elected, he was eager to fix the problems. He shored up the building and made it more sound. But the starry vault painted on the ceiling had sustained serious damage, and a crack patched with bricks and plaster ran through the sky. Julius II immediately considered enlisting Michelangelo to repaint the ceiling.

One evening in the spring of 1506, a week or two after Michelangelo had fled to Florence, the pope and Bramante, the architect of the new St. Peter's Basilica, were conversing over dinner. Also at the

This drawing from Ernst Steinmann's *Die Sixtinische Kapelle* depicts the Sistine Chapel before Michelangelo worked on it. Originally, the ceiling of the chapel was frescoed in a deep (and expensive) blue with gold stars scattered across the sky. Italian frescoists often used ground stones to achieve the deepest colors. The blue of the sky might have come from powdered lapis lazuli; the stars were real gold applied after the plaster dried.

White Smoke

Whenever a pope dies, the College of Cardinals meets in the Sistine Chapel to elect a new pope. The cardinals, the highest-level appointees within the church, are forbidden contact with the outside world during the conclave; the punishment for breaking the vow of secrecy that they take at the beginning of the meeting is excommunication.

Each cardinal receives a ballot for each round of voting, upon which he writes the name of his candidate. The ballots are then collected at the altar of the chapel in a chalice. They are tallied and burned after each vote. When there is no agreement, the ballots are mixed with straw to create black smoke; when a pope is elected, the smoke is white.

Donato Bramante devoted himself to architecture in Rome and holds the distinction as the first architect of note in the Renaissance. His choices and tastes dictated architectural fashions for more than a century.

table was Piero Rosselli, a Florentine mason and friend of Michelangelo. Rosselli would later write to Michelangelo of the conversation.

The pope informed Bramante that he would be sending the architect Giuliano da Sangallo to Florence to bring Michelangelo back to Rome. Bramante assured the pontiff that Michelangelo had no intention of taking on the project. He said Michelangelo had told him that he "did not wish to attend to anything but the tomb and not to painting."

"Holy Father," Bramante continued, "I do not think he has the courage to attempt the work, because he has small experience in painting figures, and these will be raised high above the line of vision, and in foreshortening. That is something different from painting on the ground."

Bramante knew what he was talking about when it came to painting murals, but he was a poor judge of Michelangelo's temperment and talent. It was true that Michelangelo had sold only one painting—the *Doni*

Tondo, a circular picture (*tondo* means a round frame) of the Holy Family—since leaving Ghirlandaio's workshop. But the *Doni Tondo* clearly attested to his skill. Bramante, or so Michelangelo suspected, had other motives for speaking ill of Michelangelo's skills as a painter, namely to persuade the pope to give the commision to Bramante's nephew, Raphael. Julius II was unswayed by Bramante's protests, but put the idea aside for a year while he led his armies on the campaign to regain control of the Papal States.

While Julius II waged war, Michelangelo was living simply yet comfortably in Florence. He bought a sizable farm outside of Florence that supplied him with wood, grain, olives, and grapes. He would continue to buy property throughout his life, and soon became the primary financial supporter of his entire family.

Michelangelo's Florentine contentment was disturbed when Julius II returned to Rome emboldened by his conquests in the Papal States. He and Michelangelo had reconciled in Bologna in November 1506; in May 1508, the pope called the artist to Rome to take on the ❶ **Sistine Chapel** ceiling. Reluctantly, Michelangelo agreed. The project would consume him over the next few years.

The Agony and the Ecstasy

The first task to be accomplished was the design and construction of the scaffolding that would enable the artist to reach the ceiling. Although Irving Stone's

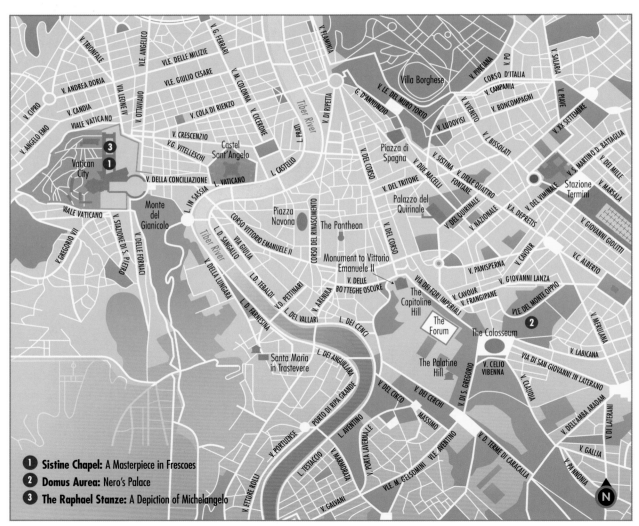

❶ **Sistine Chapel:** A Masterpiece in Frescoes
❷ **Domus Aurea:** Nero's Palace
❸ **The Raphael Stanze:** A Depiction of Michelangelo

The Domus Aurea and the Sistine Chapel

In July 64 A.D., an enormous fire raged through Rome for nine days, destroying much of the city. On the burnt land, the emperor Nero built one of the most opulent palatial complexes ever constructed, the ❷ **Domus Aurea**, or Golden House. All its walls and ceilings were painted with fanciful scenes of animals, people, mythical beasts, and lush greenery. The long walls were embellished with faux architectural elements—moldings and doorways—that divided the enormous spaces into manageable sections and provided a structure to decorate. Fourteen hundred years later, this palace would inspire the Florentine frescoists commissioned to decorate the Sistine Chapel's walls.

Over the centuries, the Domus Aurea was stripped of its gilding and jewels. Parts of it were filled in and became the foundation for other building projects. On other parts, gardens and vineyards began to grow, and cattle grazed over the site. In the mid- to late fifteenth century, the ceilings of the Domus Aurea weakened and holes opened in the hillsides. Unaware of what they had found, visitors began to frequent what they called "the grottoes," lowering themselves in through the holes in the hills.

Standing at ceiling-level on top of piles of rubble, visitors rediscovered the frescoed grandeur of Nero's palace, remarkably preserved for centuries. Artists, thrilled with the find, called the designs "grotesques" (because they thought they were in a grotto). When Lorenzo de' Medici sent Florentine frescoists to work on the Sistine Chapel in 1480, they visited the grottoes. Pietro Perugino, Sandro Botticelli, Cosimo Roselli, Luca Signorelli, and Domenico Ghirlandaio (Michelangelo's future teacher) drew inspiration from these works.

Like the painters of the Domus Aurea, the Florentine frescoists divided the long space of the Sistine Chapel's walls with faux architecture, creating form and space from a flat wall. They employed fanciful and imaginative motifs from the Domus Aurea in their paintings, and set

The Domus Aurea stretched from the Palatine Hill to the Esquiline Hill and included a lake and hunting grounds. When he moved into his lavish palace, Nero is said to have exclaimed, "At last I can live like a human being!"

the stories they were telling among the ruins of Rome and in buildings resembling the rooms of the Domus Aurea.

Their scheme for the Sistine Chapel reflected the purpose of the room. Below Piermatteo d'Amelia's blue sky was a tier of ancient popes, reminding the conclave of the historic and spiritual nature of their electoral task. Beneath the row of popes, in a band that extends all the way around the chapel, the painters depicted scenes from the lives of Moses and Jesus, the two most important figures in the Old and New Testaments. Each event from Moses's life was paired with one from Jesus's life, illustrating the parallels between their lives. The cycle continued around the chapel, with each panel facing the corresponding panel on the opposite wall. The scheme also drew connections between the Old and New Testaments, the old covenant symbolized by circumcision (*The Circumcision of Zipporah*) and the new by communion (*The Last Supper*).

novel *The Agony and the Ecstasy* presents a compelling image of Michelangelo lying on his back high above the chapel floor, the reality was probably much less dramatic.

Bramante suggested that the scaffolding be suspended from the ceiling. Rope and wood—both expensive commodities—were purchased to execute his design, but Michelangelo halted the work. How would the holes left by the suspended ropes be filled when the scaffolding was removed?

Michelangelo dismantled what had been built and designed his own scaffold. Because the materials were so expensive, he could work on only half of the chapel at once. But because his design was spare and efficient, the chapel could continue to be used while work went on. When the scaffolding was complete, the extra rope was

sold and provided a dowry for Michelangelo's carpenter's two daughters. Later, Bramante applied Michelangelo's technique when he needed scaffolding for St. Peter's.

Building the scaffolding and preparing the ceiling to be frescoed took many months, during which Michelangelo worked out his design for the ceiling. He chose to depict the history of God and man working together, and produced a scheme consisting of several interrelated components. Down the center of the vault are scenes from Genesis, starting with Noah and working backward chronologically to Creation. Sitting on thrones set into the monumental trompe l'oeil architecture are the prophets and sibyls who predicted the coming of Christ. Above the windows in triangular frames are scenes of families: mothers, fathers, and children—the human family. Finally, the lunettes

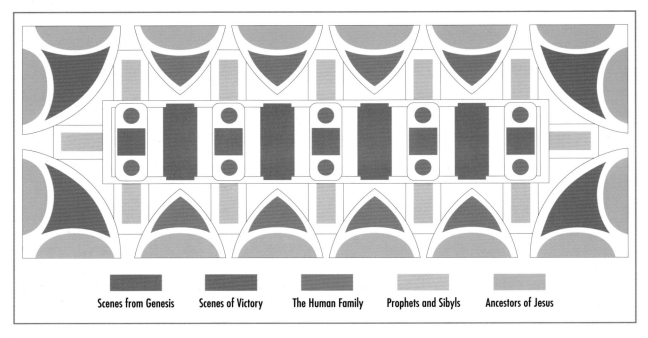

Scenes from Genesis   Scenes of Victory   The Human Family   Prophets and Sibyls   Ancestors of Jesus

above the windows (where Michelangelo's creations meet the popes) are filled with the ancestors of Jesus, establishing the lineage that runs from Moses to Christ. In each of the four corners of the room, spandrels tell stories of the victory of the Jewish people over peril. Between the primary figures, medallions, nudes, and dramatic architectural elements divide the space into regular geometric spans.

Once the design was worked out, Michelangelo prepared cartoons (full-size sketches) of the figures and architectural elements. He employed assistants, including Francesco Granacci and several other Florentine painters, to help prepare the plaster, transfer the cartoons, paint the smaller figures, and prepare his colors. Because the windows in the chapel are near the ceiling, the team had good lighting. The floor of the

Italian Fresco Technique

Fresco painting relies on techniques that have remained the same since ancient times. Because water and moisture easily damage frescoes, the art form has thrived in dry climates. Preparation of the surface is labor intensive: The surface is dampened, and the workers lay on a layer of lime plaster called *arriccio*. Once the *arriccio* has dried, the artists start work. Pigments are mixed with limewater to form a bond with the wet plaster to which they are applied, creating a hard and durable surface. Painters work in small sections called *giornata*, or "a day's work."

Each *giornata* begins with a fresh layer of plaster called *intonaco*. While the plaster is still damp, the design is transferred to it, either from cartoons or freehand. The transfer can be accomplished in two ways: by using a stylus to trace the outlines into the damp plaster, or by using pinpricks to transfer finer details with a bit of charcoal dust.

The Hall of Maps in the Vatican Museums offers a chance to take a close look at frescoes from the late sixteenth century. As the dotted lines show, cartoons were transferred using colored dust applied through perforations in paper to wet plaster. Normally, the dots were then obscured with color; in this case, the plan changed but the transfer marks remained.

Once the cartoons have been transferred, pigments—minerals ground to a very fine powder and mixed with limewater—are painted on using brushes. The brilliance of the colors and the textures created in the fresco can be manipulated by varying the amount of liquid mixed with the minerals. In some places in the Sistine Chapel, Michelangelo used almost no water, applying the pigment to the plaster with very little dilution, which created a brilliant finish.

Fresco a secco, dry fresco painting, can be used to touch up a painting once it is finished. The colors tend to flake off over time, however.

scaffolding hid the painting from viewers below and protected the floor of the chapel from falling debris, as well as preventing workers from falling to their deaths.

Much of the organization and imagery of Michelangelo's work recalls the Arch of Constantine and the Domus Aurea. The Arch of Constantine uses nude figures as decoration, much as Michelangelo uses small nude figures called *putti* as part of his design. The nudes, or *ignudi*, perform one of two functions: they hold up the ribbons "suspending" the medallions and they hold garlands of oak leaves and acorns, which are part of Julius II's family crest.

Both the *ignudi* and the prophets illustrate Michelangelo's adaptive qualities as an artist. The prophets he painted first—near the entrance wall—are classical and symmetrical. Moving across the ceiling, the figures become more and more athletic, taking on action at the end just as the *ignudi* do. Clothed and nude, floating without wings or halos, the figures illustrate his anatomical fascination.

Michelangelo applied the same techniques he used in sculpting to his painted figures. For example, he used crosshatching to create shadows, just as he did with a fine chisel on marble. For Michelangelo, his painting was most successful when he focused on the anatomy of his figures.

When the ceiling was cleaned during the late twentieth century, the *giornate* were mapped, revealing Michelangelo's progress across the vaulted ceiling. The surface of the ceiling, it turns out, is not smooth. The plaster levels change from one *giornata* to the next.

As Michelangelo worked, he encountered problems. By the time he finished *The Flood*, for example, one of the nine scenes from Genesis, the work he had completed had begun to mildew. He saw this as an opportunity to walk away from the project and return to sculpting Julius II's tomb. Julius II, however, sent Giuliano da Sangallo to advise Michelangelo. Sangallo "realized that Michelangelo had applied the plaster too wet, and consequently the dampness coming through produced that effect; and, when Michelangelo had been advised of this, he was forced to continue, and no excuse served."

Michelangelo was also bothered by the fact that the chapel continued to be used while he worked. On June 10, 1508, the papal chamberlain recorded in his diary: "In the upper part of the chapel of the building work was being done with much dust, and the workmen did not stop as I ordered. For which the cardinals complained. Although several times I reproved the workmen, they did not stop; I went to the pope who was annoyed with me because I had not admonished them and the work continued without permission, even though the pope sent two successive chamberlains who ordered them to stop, which was done with difficulty."

It wasn't just chapel services that interrupted Michelangelo's work. "While he was painting, Pope Julius often wanted to go and inspect the work; he would climb up by a ladder and Michelangelo would hold out a hand to help him up onto the scaffolding." The spandrels in the four corners of the room illustrate scenes of salvation, but the head on Judith's platter looks like that of Julius II.

The Sculptor in Rome

Michelangelo and his assistants worked for two years on the first half of the chapel, gaining speed and confidence as they proceeded. The painters completed *The Creation of Eve* in only four *giornate*, whereas *The Flood*, completed earlier, took twenty-nine *giornate*, not including a section that had to be redone because part of the fresco was destroyed and had to be reworked.

Upon descending from the scaffolding each day, Michelangelo headed home to his workshop and house at Piazza Rusticucci, where he read, worked on pieces destined for Julius II's tomb, wrote poetry, and corresponded with his family—signing many of his letters "sculptor" despite the enormous painting project he was undertaking.

Although now wealthy, Michelangelo lived a simple life, employing a modest staff of servants and cooks to maintain his household. He could have feasted sumptuously, but he enjoyed a diet much like that of the average Roman: pasta, tomatoes, bread, and wine. He probably began his day with a glass of wine and a

The Sibyls

Sibyls, or prophetesses, appear in Greek literature as far back as the fifth century B.C. Perhaps the most famous sibyl held court at Delphi, where her oracular visions became the stuff of legend. The Roman Empire imported the tradition, and sibyls could be found at Tivoli and Naples, among other places.

The sibyls Michelangelo depicts are those who predicted the coming of Jesus. Sibyls take on an important role in Renaissance art and are often depicted as women of strength and beauty. Michelangelo's sibyls are not all beautiful, but they are all powerful.

The Libyan Sibyl.

piece of bread. Before midday he would stop to take the *comestio*, a light lunch consisting of bread with a little meat, perhaps some soup, and a salad. At the end of the day, for the *prandium*, he might have indulged in a little more meat, perhaps some macaroni, and certainly more bread and wine.

Romans in Michelangelo's day frequented the small and generally inexpensive *trattoria* (neighborhood restaurant) for variety and convenience. With offerings such as pig's liver, chicken, fritters, and stews, the smells emanating from local eateries drew people inside, where gentlemen mingled with laborers and conversation flowed with the wine.

Michelangelo's personal routine was also simple. He worked late, went to church, and enjoyed his friends. His standards for hygiene were not very high, however—even for Renaissance Rome. "He constantly wore boots fashioned from dogs' skins on his bare feet for months at a time, so that when he later wanted to remove them his skin would often peel off as well."

His four brothers relied on him for financial support during much of their lives. One became a priest but was later defrocked. Two asked Michelangelo to set them up in the wool trade, which he did. His brothers also asked him to use his influence to secure positions for them in Rome.

Being away from his family was not easy for Michelangelo, but he likely savored the distance at times, for his family taxed his patience and temper. In June 1509, for instance, he chastised his brother Giovansimone: "To make it short, I can tell you for certain you haven't a thing in the world, and your spending money and household necessities are what I give you and have given you for some time now, for the love of God and thinking you were my brother like the rest. Now I know for certain you are not my brother."

For the most part, however, Michelangelo dispatched sweet words, not harsh ones, to his family. For instance, on September 15, 1509, while working on the first half of the ceiling, Michelangelo wrote his father:

> Attend to living, and let property go sooner than suffer discomforts, for I would rather have you alive and poor, because if you were dead, I wouldn't care for all the gold in the world, and if those chirping crickets there or anyone else reproves you, let them talk, for they are ignorant men and without love.

On one occasion, Michelangelo requested permission to celebrate a feast day with his family in Florence, to which Julius II replied, "Well, what about this chapel? When will it be finished?"

"When I can, Holy Father," replied Michelangelo.

Furious, the pope struck Michelangelo with a staff and roared, " 'When I can, when I can't'; I'll make you finish it myself."

Michelangelo left in a huff and prepared, once again, to return to Florence. The pope's chamberlain followed him home, bearing five hundred scudi and making excuses for the pope, "declaring that such acts were all signs of his favour and affection."

Julius II continued to hound the painter, and Michelangelo complained that the pontiff's impatience interfered with his progress. One day, when Julius II again asked when he would be done, Michelangelo replied, "When it satisfies me in its artistic details," to which the pope replied, "We want you to satisfy us in our desire to see it done quickly."

In September 1510, as work was nearing completion on the first half of the ceiling, Michelangelo's brother

Buonarroto became gravely ill. In a letter to his father, Michelangelo wrote that "if he were really bad, I would come up there by the post this next week, although it would damage me very much . . . if Buonarroto is in danger, let me know, because I shall leave everything."

Indeed, Michelangelo did "leave everything" and rush to Florence. His brother made a speedy recovery, but Michelangelo found that his father had withdrawn money from his accounts without permission. Explaining himself, his father wrote: "I said to myself, seeing your last letter, 'Michelangelo won't return for six or eight months from now and in that time I shall have returned from San Casciano.' I will sell everything and will do everything to replace what I took."

Sonnet to John of Pistoia on the Sistine Ceiling (1509–12)

I've got myself a goiter from this strain,
As water gives the cats in Lombardy
Or maybe it is in some other country;
My belly's pushed by force beneath my chin.

My beard toward Heaven, I feel the back of my brain
Upon my neck, I grow the breast of a Harpy;
My brush, above my face continually,
Makes it a splendid floor by dripping down.

My loins have penetrated to my paunch,
My rump's a crupper, as a counterweight,
And pointless the unseeing steps I go.

In front of me my skin is being stretched
While it folds up behind and forms a knot,
And I am bending like a Syrian bow.

The First Unveiling

While Michelangelo was in Florence, the pope had ventured to Bologna, where he fell ill and then proceeded to fight the French, who had advanced on the city. The first half of the ceiling was ready to be unveiled, but Julius II insisted that the scaffolding not be removed until he was in attendance. In the pope's

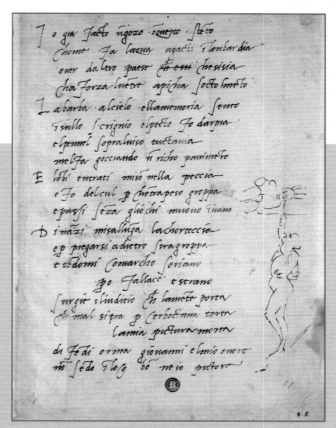

In the corner of the page on which he penned a sonnet for a friend, Michelangelo sketched himself on scaffolding, painting a figure above his head.

Raphael of Urbino (1483–1520)

Although Michelangelo seems to have been convinced that Bramante and Raphael conspired against him, it is unlikely the two colluded.

Raphael, the son of a painter as well as Bramante's nephew and student, grew up in Urbino. When he arrived in Rome—too late in 1508 to vie for the Sistine Chapel commission—he was already well-known as a painter. He used Rome as a laboratory, immersing himself in the art surrounding him, including the surviving frescoes on the walls of the Domus Aurea. He also studied Michelangelo's work whenever possible.

Raphael was soon commissioned by the pope to fresco three rooms in the Vatican used as an office and library. The ❸ **Raphael Stanze**, as they are now known, were painted between 1508 and 1511. The most famous of the rooms, the Room of Segnatura, features figures of Theology, Philosophy, Justice, and Poetry hovering on the ceiling. Wall murals illustrate ideals important to humanists like Julius II: *Parnassus* (Poetry), *The Cardinal and the Theological Virtues and the Law* (Justice), *The Disputation over the Most Holy Sacrament* (Theology), and *The School of Athens* (Philosophy).

While Michelangelo was in Florence, Bramante, who had keys to the Sistine Chapel, snuck Raphael into the chapel and up onto the scaffolding to have a look at the work in progress. After seeing the first half of Michelangelo's work in the Sistine Chapel, Raphael returned to *The School of Athens*. The fresco portrays the great thinkers of the ancient world debating and teaching. On the stairs, beneath the figures of Plato and Aristotle, Raphael chipped out the original image and applied fresh plaster, painting a morose, solitary figure slouching against a stone rail. The figure, known as the *pensieroso* ("the thinker"), wears leather boots and a cinched shirt—clothes more modern than those of any other figures—and his nose is flattened as if he had been punched long ago.

Three years after Michelangelo completed his work on the ceiling of the Sistine Chapel, Pope Leo X commissioned a series of tapestries from Raphael to run the circumference of the Sistine Chapel. For his labors, Raphael commanded a sum of 16,000 ducats—more than five times what Michelangelo had received for the chapel ceiling. The tapestries were stolen during the Sack of Rome in 1527 and were not restored until 1550. The Vatican Museums now display them under sensitive lighting to prevent fading or deterioration.

After seeing the Sistine Chapel, Raphael returned to his work *The School of Athens*. He painted Michelangelo as Heraclitus, the Greek philosopher, adding him to his pantheon of ancient scholars.

absence, work continued. Michelangelo shifted his attention to preparing drawings and cartoons for the second half of the ceiling. Although Michelangelo looked forward to the pope's return because he wanted to be paid, the pope's nine-month absence gave the artist and his team a much-needed respite. The work was taxing, and Michelangelo had developed severe eyestrain, which kept him from reading unless he tipped his head back.

In June 1511, Julius II returned to Rome. Two months later, on August 15, 1511, the pope presided over morning mass in the Sistine Chapel. Pilgrims, dignitaries, and guests thronged the chapel, as eager as the pope to see the ceiling unveiled. According to Condivi, "The opinion and the expectation which everyone had of Michelangelo brought all of Rome to see this thing, and the pope also went there before the dust raised by the dismantling of the scaffold."

The crowds were amazed by what they saw. The *Rome Pietà* had cemented Michelangelo's place as a great sculptor; the Sistine Chapel ceiling established him as a tremendous painter.

Raphael may well have been among the crowd that morning. If so, he would not have been warmly embraced by Michelangelo, for Michelangelo suspected Raphael of asking Bramante if he, Raphael, could be allowed to finish the ceiling. "This greatly disturbed Michelangelo, and before Pope Julius he gravely protested the wrong which Bramante was doing him; and in Bramante's presence he complained to the pope, unfolding to him all the persecutions he had received from Bramante."

With the scaffold out of the way, Michelangelo could finally see the work from afar. Viewed from the floor, the figures in *The Flood* disappear into the crowded scenes and the ancestors of Christ bunch together, but the prophets are strikingly powerful. With this in mind,

Michelangelo decided that the second half of the ceiling would feature fewer figures in each scene and that, like the prophets in the first half, those figures would be larger and the intensity of their actions more pronounced.

The first scene Michelangelo took on in the second half proved to be his most celebrated: *The Creation of Adam*. Accomplished in just two or three weeks, the scene features two suspended figures with very little scenery to anchor them.

Whereas the lunettes in the first half were painted in three or four days, the artists' pace increased as they moved across the ceiling; the work labeled *Roboam Abias* was accomplished in a single *giornata*. Michelangelo was probably impatient to finish, especially because Julius II was not in good health. The death of the pope could mean financial headaches.

The images of God in the Sistine Chapel show Michelangelo's transformation as he worked across the ceiling. In *The Creation of Eve*, God looks like a philosopher in Raphael's *The School of Athens*. Dressed in robes and standing firmly on the ground, he assumes a human form. But the figure of God in *The Creation of Adam* soars through the air, loosely draped, with bare feet and powerful muscles. And the God who appears in *The Separation of Light from Darkness* takes on Zeus's qualities, with a strong physique rippling under his loose garment.

The Desired End

In July 1512, Michelangelo complained to his brother Buonarroto: "I work harder than anyone who ever lived. I am not well, and worn out with this stupendous labour, and yet I am patient in order to achieve the desired end." Julius II was not so patient and, despite battling ill health and the threat posed by French forces

Michelangelo painted the scenes from Genesis in reverse chronological order. As he gained confidence and observed his work from the floor, he created larger and more dramatic figures.

in the northern Papal States, he continued to harass the painter to finish.

Finally, on October 31, 1512, the chapel's doors were opened and Romans flocked to see the wonders therein. Michelangelo's work created an immediate sensation in the city and beyond. In covering the enormous space with a program of panels and tremendous figures, Michelangelo had solved the problem of perspective that faces many muralists. The ceiling is impossible to see all at once, even though it soars sixty feet above the floor. No seat in the chapel has a better view than another—and all views are beautiful.

Julius II, pleased with Michelangelo's work as well as with the hubbub it had created, showered the artist with gifts. However, Michelangelo never felt he was fairly compensated for his work, and he complained bitterly. For his part, Julius II, seeking to make his monument even grander, approached the artist about adding gold and ultramarine to the figures. He asked Michelangelo to reassemble the scaffolding and add sparkle because without it, he said, "It will look poor." Michelangelo, reluctant to incur more expenses and to rebuild the scaffolding, replied, "Those who are depicted there, they were poor too."

With Julius II's death in 1513, Michelangelo could have been forgiven for thinking he would no longer be pestered by the pope about the Sistine Chapel. And, indeed, that was the case for no fewer than twenty-three years. But in 1536, he would be called back to the chapel again, this time to paint the altar wall for a very different kind of pope.

projects, he selected a second block of marble and began the work again. The sculpture took three years to complete and was installed in March 1521.

The contract for the piece called for "a marble Christ, large as life, nude." The concept of Jesus in the nude shows the powerful influence of ancient art:

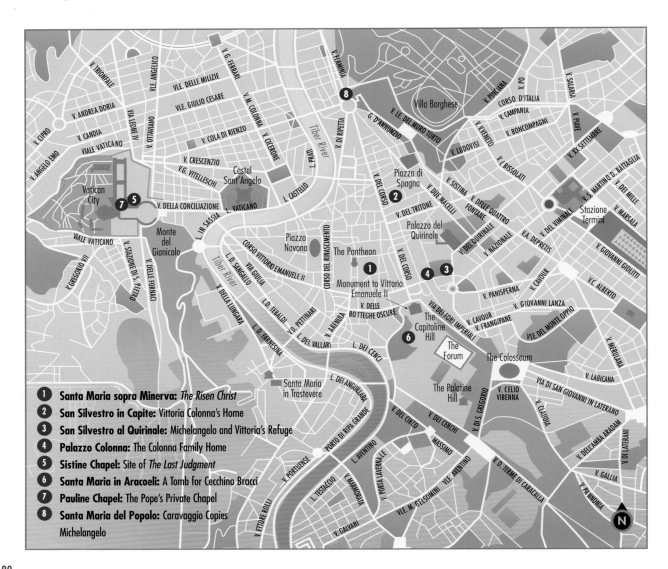

1. **Santa Maria sopra Minerva:** *The Risen Christ*
2. **San Silvestro in Capite:** Vittoria Colonna's Home
3. **San Silvestro al Quirinale:** Michelangelo and Vittoria's Refuge
4. **Palazzo Colonna:** The Colonna Family Home
5. **Sistine Chapel:** Site of *The Last Judgment*
6. **Santa Maria in Aracoeli:** A Tomb for Cecchino Bracci
7. **Pauline Chapel:** The Pope's Private Chapel
8. **Santa Maria del Popolo:** Caravaggio Copies Michelangelo

indeed, Christ looks like classical images of Apollo. Squeamish clergy later added a gilded loincloth to the figure, which remains today.

As with *Moses* and *David*, Michelangelo manipulated the figure's proportions to his own purposes, but this manipulation has raised criticism because the intentions of the distortion are not immediately obvious. The figure appears to be disproportional from several angles, with a large torso and skinny legs; from behind, it looks misshapen. But when viewed from the left, the sculpture comes into focus. Jesus's stance forces the cross to the forefront, and his body disappears behind it. Unfinished patches on the back of the sculpture indicate that Michelangelo did not intend for the viewer to see Christ's back.

Michelangelo showed keen awareness of lighting and placement as a sculptor and as an architect. The natural lighting in Santa Maria sopra Minerva is dim and angled, coming from high windows. Critics argue that Michelangelo planned *The Risen Christ* using his understanding of light effects. Contemporary sketches show that *The Risen Christ* was originally placed in a niche in the wall to be seen from one viewpoint. The niche, representing the tomb, allows the sculpture to emerge from "the shadow of death" and directs the viewer to the most proportional view of the piece.

Michelangelo's contemporaries adored the work. The painter Sebastiano del Piombo wrote that "the knees of that figure are worth all of Rome." Indeed, the sculpture became an object venerated and adored by the faithful. Jesus's foot, stroked and kissed for centuries, has at times been covered by a brass slipper to keep it from wearing away. Michelangelo's patron Metello Vari was so pleased with the final product that he presented the artist with a horse. Yet, in the

By depicting Jesus in Rome in *The Risen Christ* (1518–21), Michelangelo emphasized the connection between the political and the spiritual center of the church—reaffirming the mandate of the popes.

Santa Maria sopra Minerva, just a block from the Pantheon, sits on a site where a temple to Minerva once stood. Sculptures, frescoes, oil paintings, and tombs (including those of Popes Leo X and Clement VII) are crowded into small chapels lining the nave.

position it now occupies, *The Risen Christ* is easily overlooked among the other pieces in the sanctuary.

Back to Florence

Florentine Leo X wanted to leave his mark on his hometown, so he commissioned Michelangelo to return there. Commissions and then politics kept Michelangelo in Florence for nearly two decades. He completed *The Risen Christ* in Florence, sending it with his assistant, Pietro Urbino, to be installed in Rome. Many blame Urbino for "ruining" the work because he was charged

with finishing the details and installing the sculpture.

While Michelangelo was living in Florence, Rome suffered a period of political turmoil and violence that left the city battered and bruised. Attempting to stifle the growing power of the Reformation, inspired by Martin Luther in Germany, Leo X aligned himself with Charles V, who was both king of Spain and Holy Roman Emperor. At that time, the Holy Roman Empire consisted of not just the Netherlands and much of Germany but also much of southern Italy, including Naples, Sicily, and Sardinia. Charles V was a bitter foe of the Reformation, which was finding allies among German princes eager to assert their independence from the Holy Roman Empire. He was also locked in a fight with France for domination of Europe, and he viewed Italy as the key to winning that struggle. But the French had allies in much of northern Italy, and in 1524, Pope Clement VII switched sides and joined the French, hoping to check Charles V's grab for power.

In response, Charles V sent an army to Rome. When his troops arrived on May 6, 1527, they had not been paid in months; their leader, the Constable of Bourbon, was killed at the city gates. Desperate, furious, and leaderless, the troops abandoned the rules of warfare and ravaged the city. The streets were filled with the bodies of civilians as soldiers advanced through the city, neighborhood by neighborhood. By nightfall, Spanish troops had taken Piazza Navona and Germans held Campo dei Fiori.

The invading troops, many of whom were Lutheran, searched for cardinals and religious booty; they also committed terrible atrocities. Women and children were raped. Food stores and homes were burned. Rotting bodies littered the streets while terrified families barricaded themselves in their homes for weeks. Others fled to the countryside. To the troops, works of art represented the arrogance and excess of the papacy; as they rampaged through the city, they destroyed an untold number of priceless pieces. The stained glass from France that Bramante had designed for the new St. Peter's Basilica was among the casualties.

Many of Rome's artists joined the exodus from the city. Some, however, were not so lucky as to escape. In the midst of the siege, Francesco Mazzola, known as Parmigianino, was at work painting an image of Saint Jerome. German troops stormed in, threatening to kill him. The artist persuaded them to take his pens and drawings as a ransom for his life. Vincenzo da San Gimignano, another painter, became violently depressed. Visions of the horrors he witnessed rendered him unable to work, and he eventually took his own life.

Fortunately for Michelangelo, he had secured a plum commission in Florence: the Laurentian Library at San Lorenzo. He was at work on this commission when Charles V sacked Rome. For the next seven years he would work steadily on civic projects in Florence. His grandest commissions came at the hands of the papacy and the Medici family, and Michelangelo often found himself perched precariously as the papacy changed hands

Charles V's army plunders Rome in 1527.

between families. When the Medici were in control, Michelangelo had more work than he could manage. But when their fortunes and funds ran low, he had to position himself carefully to secure other commissions. Because Michelangelo was a republican, Florence became an unfriendly place for him in the mid-1530s. After Alessandro de' Medici assumed the role of tyrant and expelled the last of the old republican government, Michelangelo joined the ranks of Florentine expatriates. In 1534, he left Florence, never to return.

A Cadre of Friends

Michelangelo has sometimes been painted as a stingy, friendless genius, too busy with work to maintain relationships. In 1509, while painting the Sistine Chapel, he wrote to his brother Buonarroto, "I live here in great toil and great weariness of body, and have no friends of any kind and don't want any, and haven't the time to eat what I need."

Michelangelo focused most of his energies on his art. A friend once remarked, "It's a pity you haven't taken a wife, for you would have had many children and bequeathed to them many honorable works." Michelangelo replied, "I have too much of a wife in this art that has always afflicted me, and the works I shall leave behind will be my children, and even if they are nothing, they will live for a long while."

In addition, over the years, Michelangelo developed a reputation for having a temper—his *terribilità*. Some acquaintances considered him arrogant; others found him eccentric, even bizarre. Yet he was fiercely loyal to those who won his respect. His relationships crossed socioeconomic, gender, and age boundaries to include members of the nobility and the privileged clergy, writers and fellow artists, men and women, and those older and those younger than himself. Many of Michelangelo's friendships spanned decades.

His relationships with his employees were also long-lasting. Michelangelo kept careful records of their names, wages, and the projects on which they worked. Many stayed with him for years. He paid them well, provided them with housing, and was involved in all aspects of their lives. His generosity helped ensure their loyalty and afforded him a stable workforce, committed to the quality he valued and familiar with his working style. He provided the basic tools they needed: benches, rulers, stools, and a smith to sharpen their tools. They, in turn, carried out his work and upheld his exacting standards. Many of his employees earned nicknames revealing their personalities or physiques and their employer's affections for them: the She-Cat, Knobby, Fats, the Anti-Christ, and Little Liar.

When Michelangelo met the young artist Tommaso de' Cavalieri (c. 1518–87), a handsome Roman gentleman with good breeding and a good education, he found a kindred spirit. Although Michelangelo was fifty-seven years old when they met, he presented the younger man with poetry and drawings. He wrote a letter from

Sonnet to Tommaso de' Cavalieri (1533)

Since through the eyes the heart's seen in the face,
I have no other way so evident
To show my flame; let this then be sufficient,
O my dear Lord, to ask you now for grace.

Perhaps your spirit, gazing at this chaste
Fire that consumes me, will, more than I credit,
Have trust, and be with me speedy and lenient,
As grace abounds for him who well entreats.

O happy that day, if this is true!
Then at one instant in their ancient road
The house will be stopped, time, sun, the days,

That I may have, though it is not my due,
My so much desired, my so sweet lord,
In my unworthy ready arms for always.

Florence, touchingly awed that Cavalieri had responded to his tokens: "If it is really true that you feel within as you write me outwardly, as to your judging my works, if it should happen that one of them as I wish should please you, I shall much sooner call it lucky than good."

Cavalieri, a charming man, assumed the role of younger companion. He wrote, "I promise you, indeed, that from me you will receive an equal, and maybe a greater exchange, who never cared for any man more than for you, nor ever wanted any friendship more than yours; and if in nothing else, at least in this I have very good judgment." The relationship between the two men sparked new bursts of creativity in both as they exchanged letters, poems, and drawings.

Much has been made of Michelangelo's relationship with Cavalieri; some biographers have cast them as lovers. Perhaps they were. His verses written for Cavalieri do not differ much from those written for other friends—men and women—but they show an intense devotion and love. Given Michelangelo's spirituality and his increasing devotion to a pious life, he may have spent his energies in chaste adoration—whatever his sexual preferences were. Michelangelo's poetry for Cavalieri hints at desire but also reflects the ideas of Platonic love, which he embraced as he aged.

Cavalieri remained friends with Michelangelo until Michelangelo died, and Michelangelo left some of his projects in Cavalieri's hands, including the completion of his redesign of the Campidoglio.

Vittoria Colonna: A Friend in Faith

In 1536, Michelangelo met another kindred spirit: Vittoria Colonna, the Marchese of Pescara, who had married at nineteen and was widowed by thirty-five. She mourned the death of her husband intensely and wrote scores of poems expressing her sorrow. Rather

When Vittoria Colonna died in 1547, Michelangelo grieved deeply. Condivi wrote, "She often traveled to Rome from Viterbo and other places where she had gone for recreation and to spend the summer, prompted by no other reason than to see Michelangelo; and he in return bore her so much love that I remember hearing him say that his only regret was that, when he went to see her as she was departing from this life, he did not kiss her forehead or her face as he kissed her hand. On account of her death he remained a long time in despair and as if out of his mind."

than marrying again, as her brothers wished, Colonna devoted her life to works of charity and intellectual pursuits, which brought her to Rome, where she made Michelangelo's acquaintance.

Colonna made her home in Rome at ❷ **San Silvestro in Capite,** occupying a room in the adjoining convent. She had the ear of Rome's most powerful men, and she was not afraid to wield her influence. Her relationship with Michelangelo flowered, and soon Michelangelo, Colonna, and Cavalieri were enjoying each other's company regularly.

Michelangelo and Colonna exchanged poems and met on Sundays at ❸ **San Silvestro al Quirinale,** just down the road from the Piazza del Quirinale, for afternoon talks on the terrace. Their conversations often revolved around theological and philosophical questions; both the artist and the widow struggled with questions raised by the Reformation and the Counter-Reformation.

A Personal Theology

Michelangelo's devotion to the nude and the human body drew criticism and allegations of immorality. Like Plato, Michelangelo saw the contemplation of the human body and human beauty as a means to contemplation of divine beauty—the ultimate form hidden by flesh. Condivi wrote,

San Silvestro in Capite, on Piazza San Silvestro.

I have often heard Michelangelo converse and discourse on the subject of love and have later heard from those who were present that what he said about love was no different than what we read in the writings of Plato . . . In all my long and intimate acquaintance with Michelangelo, I have never heard any but the most honorable words cross his lips, such as have the power to extinguish in the young any unseemly and unbridled desire which might spring up. And that no foul thoughts could have arisen in his mind is evident also from the fact that he loved not only human beauty but everything beautiful in general: a beautiful horse, a beautiful dog, a beautiful landscape, a beautiful plant, a beautiful mountain, a beautiful forest, and every place and thing which is beautiful and rare of its kind, admiring them all with marveling love and selecting beauty from nature as the bees gather honey from flowers, to use it later in his works.

Spirituality was as much a part of Michelangelo's creative life as it was part of his intellectual and social life. He felt that his creative process was a result of what Plato called *furor divinus*, or divine madness—Michelangelo called it a "seizure of the soul"—in which God takes hold of the body and allows the soul to experience divinity.

An artist, Michelangelo wrote, "must maintain a good life, and if possible be holy, so that his intellect can be inspired by the Holy Spirit." When a friend asserted that God wanted Michelangelo to be an artist, he replied that he was nothing but "a poor man and of little value, a man who goes along laboring in that art which God has given me for as long as I possibly can."

Michelangelo believed that God revealed himself in glimpses and that the intention of all work should be the glorification of God through the use of one's talents in an effort to attain greater communion with God.

This Christian application of Plato's Allegory of the Cave and other theories gained popularity during the Renaissance, and Michelangelo's circle of friends would often debate these ideas.

Michelangelo designed the tabernacle behind the altar at San Silvestro in Capite; it holds the relics of St. John the Baptist as well as the *vera-imago*, a cloth with the image of Christ's face. Vittoria Colonna arranged for Michelangelo to view the cloth while he was painting *The Last Judgment*.

Madrigal to Vittoria Colonna

A man, a god rather, inside a woman,
Through her mouth has his speech,
And this has made me such
I'll never again be mine after I listen.
Ever since she has stolen
Me from myself, I'm sure,
Outside myself I'll give myself my pity.
Her beautiful features summon
Upward from false desire,
So that I see death in all other beauty.
You who bring souls, O Lady,
Through fire and water to felicity,
See to it I do not return to me.

Michelangelo studied the Old and New Testaments and developed a deep familiarity with the Scriptures. He also read the works of great theologians. Images and stories from antiquity infused his perspective on religion; the Virgin and the sibyl, the putto and the infant Jesus, Christ and Apollo took interchangeable forms. A devout Catholic, Michelangelo believed in the power of personal prayer and asked that others pray for him. He and Colonna both also believed in

The Reformation

In December 1510 two Germans from an Augustinian monastery entered Rome. One was a twenty-seven-year-old monk from Erfurt named Martin Luther. When Luther arrived at Porta del Popolo, he prostrated himself, declaring, "Blessed be Thou, holy Rome!"

Much of Luther's time in Rome is the subject of legend. Did he hear the voice of God as he climbed the steps of the Scala Santa in the Lateran Palace? Perhaps. But the seeds of what would become the Reformation were definitely sown on that trip. Luther was appalled by the casual—and sometimes irreverent—attitudes Rome's clerics displayed, and later accused priests of celebrating mass in a "slapdash fashion." While the casual bearing of the clergy offended him, the fact that some were homosexual and many had syphilis infuriated him. He was also angered by Rome's rampant poverty, prostitution, and pollution. He was taken ill while there, and blamed his sickness on the dirty air of the filthy city.

While in Rome, Martin Luther observed the construction of the new St. Peter's Basilica. Seven years later he would post his "Ninety-Five Theses"—objections, in part, to the fundraising tactics employed by the Vatican to pay for the enormous building project—and launch what we now know as the Reformation. Begun as an attempt to reform the Roman Catholic Church, the Reformation would end with the division of Western Christianity into the Catholic and Protestant churches.

Martin Luther.

As a priest, Luther longed for a less political and more transparent institution. He wrote prolifically about his ideas for change; thanks to the printing press, his words traveled quickly throughout Europe. But he was viewed in Rome not as a reformer but as a heretic. He was tried and eventually excommunicated for railing against the church. Yet, some German princes liked Luther's teachings. Eager to be out from under the pope's thumb, they became Protestant principalities, offering Luther safe haven and providing a fertile ground in which the Reformation could develop and grow.

the power of good works and charity—ideas that in their day smacked of Lutheranism.

As a testament to their intellectual pairing, the artist celebrated Colonna in many poems as a woman with whom he could match wits and explore ideas.

Michelangelo made several drawings for his friend, including a pietà and a crucifixion. Of the crucifixion, Colonna requested the addition of a few angels à la Raphael, to which Michelangelo objected, but he sketched them in anyway. The note accompanying the drawing of the crucifixion vowed, "I have wished to do more for you than for any man I ever knew in the world; but the great business in which I have been and am has not allowed me to let your ladyship know this." He designed a tabernacle at the Basilica di San Silvestro in Capite—her residence—perhaps in her honor or at her request.

Galleria Colonna

Vittoria Colonna's extended family owned seven palazzi in Rome in the sixteenth century. The most famous sits at the intersection of Via Quattro Novembre and Via della Pilotta: the ❹ Palazzo Colonna.

Little mention was made of Colonna in the family home; she never actually lived there. But in a corner of the Sala della Colonna Bellica (Room of the Battle Column) is a portrait of a beautiful woman in a green gown. The painting, by Bartolomeo Cancellieri, is thought to be of Colonna.

The room may look familiar to film buffs, for this is where Audrey Hepburn held court in the final scenes of *Roman Holiday* as she expressed her love for Rome and for her host, played by Gregory Peck.

The Last Judgment

Pope Paul III had long admired Michelangelo's talent, so when he was elected to the papacy in 1534, the pope immediately called the artist to the Vatican. He wanted Michelangelo to return to the ❺ Sistine Chapel, this time to paint *The Last Judgment* on the wall above the altar. Michelangelo tried to decline, citing his continued involvement with Julius II's tomb, but the pope would not hear it. "I have had this desire for thirty years, and now that I am Pope, am I not to satisfy it? I will tear up this contract, and, in any case, I intend to have you serve me!"

While awaiting Michelangelo's arrival in Rome, Michelangelo's friend Sebastiano del Piombo prepared the wall for the project, but he prepped it for an oil painting, not a fresco, and did not consult with Michelangelo. When Michelangelo found out, he flew into a rage, declaring that only women and lazy people painted in oils. He installed a new wall at an angle that allowed for ventilation, preventing an accumulation of dust on the fresco. In May 1536, Michelangelo began work—twenty-three years after completing his first venture in the same room.

The addition of *The Last Judgment* changed the focus of the Sistine Chapel significantly, directing attention to the altar wall. To install his commission, Michelangelo had to destroy two frescoes in the *Moses* and *Jesus* cycles: *The Finding of Moses* and *The Adoration of the Shepherds*, both by Perugino. In addition, two of Michelangelo's own lunettes were destroyed, along with images of several popes and the altarpiece, also designed by Perugino.

Unlike the other frescoes in the chapel, *The Last Judgment* lacks a frame and a fixed viewpoint. The wall looks as if the chapel is open to the sky, essentially

Michelangelo studied the works of Dante Alighieri (1265–1321), a Florentine poet. Dante's influence is especially powerful in Michelangelo's vision of Hell. Like Dante, Michelangelo blends the stories of Greek mythology, including characters such as Charon and Minos, with Christian concepts of salvation and damnation.

creating an enormous "window" through which the scene is seen. Michelangelo's Christ, an Apollo-like figure set off in a golden haze, moves actively, saving souls. He looks downward, wounded hand raised as if ready to swoop up a person to bring to his side. Mary, already saved, looks about her at the company of saved souls.

In most paintings of the last judgment by Renaissance artists, characters headed to Heaven wear expressions of pleasure and piety—as if they deserve to be saved. The figures of the saved in Michelangelo's version are strikingly different. Michelangelo presents the miracle of salvation according to Catholicism: no one deserves to be saved because all are sinners, yet the faithful are saved. Some of the saved wear expressions of fear and confusion, and the faces of the damned bear the surprise and sorrow of their fate. But Michelangelo's most important theological statement appears at the top of the composition: figures bearing the symbols of the Passion (the cross, the crown of thorns). The moment depicted reminds the viewer not just of the promise of being saved but of the means (Christ's crucifixion) by which Catholics believe that salvation is possible. Michelangelo's composition becomes not a warning against sin and damnation but a treatise on grace and salvation.

Michelangelo filled his depiction with nudes, something that would bring criticism for the remainder of his life. Time and again, Michelangelo maintained that physical beauty reflects spiritual and moral beauty. Yet he also distinguished between artificial and physical beauty. No clothes—no matter how grand—could disguise a sinful soul.

Known to be a shabby dresser, Michelangelo put little stock in outward frills. For example, a priest Michelangelo knew arrived one day "dressed in buckles and silk." Michelangelo wryly commented, "Oh, you

do look fine! If you were as fine on the inside as I see you are on the outside, it would be good for your soul." He filled his Heaven with gorgeous, muscular bodies, largely unfettered by the human constraints of clothing; meanwhile, the bodies of the damned writhe and wrinkle in ugly decay. Their bodies, not their clothes, reflect the condition of their souls.

When he erected the scaffolding in the Sistine Chapel for the first time, Michelangelo had been a young man. But much had changed since 1508. As he worked on *The Last Judgment*, he was keenly aware of his own aging body and the toll his work had taken on it. At sixty-five, when he had almost completed the fresco, Michelangelo fell from the scaffolding and hurt his leg. He hid away in his home in intense pain. After a few days a physician friend, Baccio Rontini, broke in and found him "in desperate shape." Rontini cared for his friend until he healed and could return to work.

Michelangelo rewarded some of his loyal friends and enemies with immortality. *The Last Judgment* is filled with likenesses of those familiar to him, some flattering and some less so. St. Sebastian, a beautiful heroic figure holding a brace of arrows, may be Tommaso de' Cavalieri. Urbino, Michelangelo's faithful assistant,

The Restoration of the Sistine Chapel
The frescoes of the Sistine Chapel received a thorough cleaning and restoration between 1979 and 1999. The cleaning process removed centuries of smoke residue and varnish, which had obscured and darkened Michelangelo's work. Although some art historians argued that the darker patina was historically correct, the cleaning process revealed the same brilliant and bold use of color that Michelangelo's contemporaries had applauded.

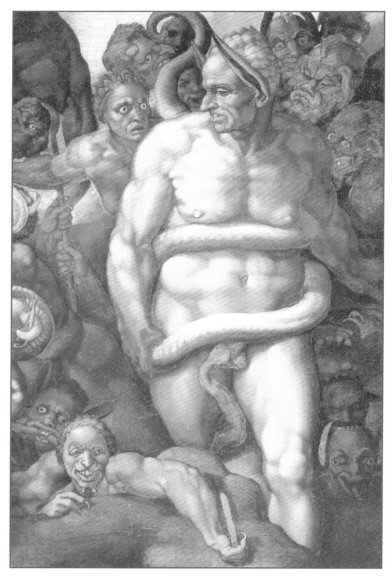

In Greek mythology, Minos is the judge of the underworld. In *The Last Judgment,* he has the face of Cesena, who disagreed with Michelangelo's portrayals of nudes.

appears as St. James. St. Peter, according to some, bears the features of Pope Paul III, an appropriate homage.

Two portraits in particular stand out. One is of Biagio da Cesena, the chamberlain of the Sistine Chapel. Cesena came with Paul III to see the painting in progress. When the pope asked what he thought of the work, Cesena said that he disapproved of nudes in holy places. In response to this remark, Michelangelo painted Cesena's face with donkey ears to represent Minos in Hell. Positioned prominently above a doorway, a snake wraps around Minos's body and swallows his penis. When Cesena complained to the pope about the depiction, Paul III reportedly replied that he could have helped, had Michelangelo put him in Purgatory, but he could do nothing for those in Hell.

The other striking portrait is of Pietro Aretino, whose features are given to St. Bartholomew. Aretino was an art critic, and the portrait may have intended to assuage Aretino's anger with Michelangelo. Aretino had written Michelangelo in 1537 requesting drawings and making suggestions for *The Last Judgment.* Michelangelo paid little attention to Aretino, which infuriated the critic, for Aretino wanted to be made a cardinal and he hoped to use a close association with the artist to win the respect of the other cardinals.

When the painting was unveiled, Aretino—like many other Romans—was scandalized that Michelangelo had filled an altar wall with nudes. "Is it possible," he asked Michelangelo in a letter of November 1545, "that you, who as a divine being do not condescend to the society of men, should have done such a thing in the foremost temple of God? Above the main altar of Jesus?" He continued, "I, in lascivious and immodest subject matter, not only use restrained and polite words, but tell my story in pure and blameless language. But you, in a subject matter of such exalted history, show angels and saints, the former without any of the decency proper to this world, and the latter lacking any of the loveliness of Heaven." *The Last Judgment* "would be appropriate in a voluptuous whorehouse, not in a supreme choir." Aretino concluded with veiled threats of exposing "Tomai"—perhaps an effort at blackmailing Michelangelo, for he still wanted drawings from him.

Even after penning such a strident letter, Aretino had the gall to write again, requesting Michelangelo to let him have "some of the drawings with which you are prodigal to the flames but so miserly to me."

Reactions

According to Giorgio Vasari, Julius II had intended for the artist to paint *The Last Judgment*—complete with nudes—over the altar of the Sistine Chapel and the *Fall of the Rebel Angels* on the back wall. In the days of Julius II, the classical nude exemplified perfection in art. But attitudes about art had changed since Julius's death. The Reformation—and the equally fierce Counter-Reformation, with

St. Bartholomew, who was skinned alive, is usually portrayed carrying his own skin. In *The Last Judgment,* the face on the skin is that of Michelangelo.

which the papacy and its allies fought back against Protestantism—unleashed a tide of puritanism. No longer was the classical and antique revered; nudity, once considered beautiful, was now deemed indecent.

Michelangelo anticipated that his art might suffer in such a censorious climate:

> *The evil, foolish and invidious mob*
> *May point, and charge to others its own taste,*
> *And yet no less my faith, my honest wish,*
> *My love and my keen longing leave me glad.*

The fact that Michelangelo did not make a physical distinction between the saved and the fallen also opened him up for criticism. Halos and wings had become the fashion of the day—such signs of salvation helped to emphasize the hierarchy some clung to as the salvation of a troubled church.

On October 31, 1541, Paul III unveiled *The Last Judgment*—twenty-nine years to the day from the first revelation of Michelangelo's work in the chapel. Whereas people had marveled at Michelangelo's work on the ceiling (the nude figure of Adam had been acclaimed as a triumph), *The Last Judgment* garnered mixed reviews primarily because most of the figures in it were nude.

Luigi del Riccio

One of Michelangelo's closest friends, Luigi del Riccio, cared for him in 1544 and 1545 when Michelangelo fell ill. Michelangelo wrote to a nephew, "I have not found a better man than him to do my business, or more faithful."

Del Riccio had adopted a young relative named Cecchino Bracci, who, in 1544, died at the age of sixteen. Michelangelo soothed his grieving friend with poems and further honored his friend's grief by designing a tomb for Bracci, installed in ❺ **Santa Maria in Aracoeli**, a church just off the Piazza del Campidoglio on the Capitoline Hill. One of Rome's most ancient basilicas, Santa Maria in Aracoeli sparkles with the light of many crystal chandeliers, invoking the vision of the heavens for which it is named.

Michelangelo wrote forty-eight epitaphs, a sonnet, and a madrigal about the death of young Cecchino Bracci, as well as designing this tomb for the teenager. His assistant Urbino made and installed it.

Michelangelo was not the only one who remembered and revered the power of the nude, and his fresco provided a powerful example for those who strove for anatomical accuracy. Thanks to printing presses, copies of *The Last Judgment* were available far and wide in a relatively short time. Soon the work was held up as a "school for artists"—a textbook of sorts, offering artists a wide range of figures to study and to copy. When Michelangelo saw painters copying his work, he mourned, "Oh, how many men this work of mine wishes to destroy!"

Although artists sought to imitate the work, most critics tried to excoriate it. Michelangelo was even attacked by those he considered his friends. Many within Vittoria Colonna's circle of intellectuals and theologians accused Michelangelo of heresy.

Paul III did not forcefully defend Michelangelo, but he did not condemn the painting either. His successors, however, were more vocal. Paul IV (1555–59) even considered destroying the Sistine Chapel and other "immodest" works of art as a means to improve public morals.

Calls to censor or destroy the Sistine Chapel's nudes would plague Michelangelo for the remainder of his life. He remained steadfast in defense of his work, however. When asked to amend the fresco, he replied defiantly, "Tell the pope that this is a small matter and can easily be amended; let him amend the world and pictures will soon amend themselves."

With the election of Pius IV (1559–65), the calls for censorship found a sympathetic pontifical ear. In 1563, twenty-two years after *The Last Judgment* was unveiled, the Council of Trent took up a discussion of art, specifically Michelangelo's frescoes. On January 21, 1564, the council ordered that the frescoes be changed.

But Michelangelo had loyal friends in the Curia (the Vatican's political administration). The eighty-nine-year-old artist was dying, so they chose Michelangelo's student, Daniele da Volterra, to make the changes, and allowed him to wait until after the artist's death.

First Volterra made alterations—painting drapery over key figures and clothes on others. Then, rather than clothing St. Catherine and St. Blaise, Volterra destroyed them and painted new, clothed figures. He sought to preserve the intention and spirit of his master's work while pleasing the squeamish clergy. For his pains, Volterra was known forever after as "the breeches maker." Volterra was not the last painter to alter *The Last Judgment*. Several popes over the centuries appointed painters to make changes, though over time the fresco suffered more from smoke damage and neglect.

The Private Chapel

Despite the controversy over *The Last Judgment*, Michelangelo continued to receive papal commissions. Paul III wanted a new private chapel. The ❼ **Pauline Chapel** is buried within the Vatican complex and is hardly known to the public—or even to scholars. For the pope, however, it is a private place of worship and is used regularly. The art Michelangelo created for Paul III's commission turned out to be his last frescoes: *The Crucifixion of Saint Peter* and *The Conversion of Saul*.

In scale, the project cannot compare to *The Last Judgment* or the ceiling of the Sistine Chapel. Michelangelo began work in November 1542. His progress was delayed by illness in the summer of 1544, but he completed the *Conversion* in 1545—the same year he finished installing the tomb of Julius II. His progress in the Pauline Chapel was further slowed by

The Crucifixion of Saint Peter (1546–50).

his appointment as architect for both St. Peter's Basilica and the Palazzo Farnese, but he finally finished the frescoes in 1550, at the age of seventy-five.

In 1549, as he worked in the Pauline Chapel, Michelangelo wrote, "Painting is to be considered the better the more it approaches relief, and relief is to be considered the worse the more it approaches painting; and therefore I used to feel that sculpture was the lantern of painting and that there was the difference between them that there is between the sun and moon." His frescoes attempt to bring painting closer to sculpture. They focus on dramatic events with little in the background to ground the figures. Like the *Rome Pietà*, the frescoes tell the story of moments.

In *The Crucifixion of Saint Peter* (1546–50) Michelangelo chooses the moment of agony as the cross is being raised and Peter lays suspended across the space in twisted pain, his face contorted and pleading. In *The Conversion of Saul*, the Holy Spirit suddenly grips Saul, traveling along a road, and his name and his path in life change forever. The *Conversion* also emphasizes the emotion of a moment—the moment when Saul converts. He is struck by fear and is overpowered by God.

At the height of the Reformation, Michelangelo chose subjects that affirmed the legitimacy of the papacy and its ties to Rome: Peter and Paul, the spiritual guardians of Rome, both of whom were martyred in the Eternal City.

Perhaps because Michelangelo presented such bare compositions, the Pauline Chapel frescoes stirred neither controversy nor adulation. After Michelangelo's death, drapes were added to some of the nudes, but the frescoes were largely ignored as the work of an elderly, doddering artist. Because of its location deep in the private areas of the papal complex, the Pauline Chapel is rarely open to the public. In 2004, the Vatican announced that Michelangelo's frescoes were being cleaned and restored using the same techniques that proved successful in the Sistine Chapel.

Caravaggio's *Crucifixion* and *Conversion*

Relatively little is known about Michelangelo Merisi da Caravaggio (1571–1610). Working in Rome, Caravaggio created dramatic and intimate scenes, drawing on the pieces that surrounded him. In the ❶ church of **Santa Maria del Popolo** (off the Piazza del Popolo, north of the Spanish Steps), Caravaggio created the same pairing of subjects that Michelangelo did for the Pauline Chapel. Unlike the Pauline Chapel, Santa Maria del Popolo is relatively easy to visit.

Caravaggio's *Crucifixion of Saint Peter* (1600–01) draws deeply from Michelangelo's work—the two Peters take the same position and have strikingly similar features. The compositions are similar, but Caravaggio takes a much darker view of the scene. His *Conversion on the Way to Damascus* (1601), however, differs markedly from Michelangelo's. Saul (who later became St. Paul), a Pharisee, was traveling on the road when he was suddenly converted to Christianity. Where Michelangelo illustrates a crowded scene with Christ in the sky performing the conversion, Caravaggio depicts Saul struck from his horse and bathed in light. In both *Crucifixion* and *Conversion*, Caravaggio makes significant use of chiaroscuro (using light and dark to achieve depth in painting). Although Michelangelo and other Renaissance artists understood chiaroscuro, painters of the seventeeth and eighteenth centuries, such as Caravaggio and Rembrandt, perfected and exploited the technique.

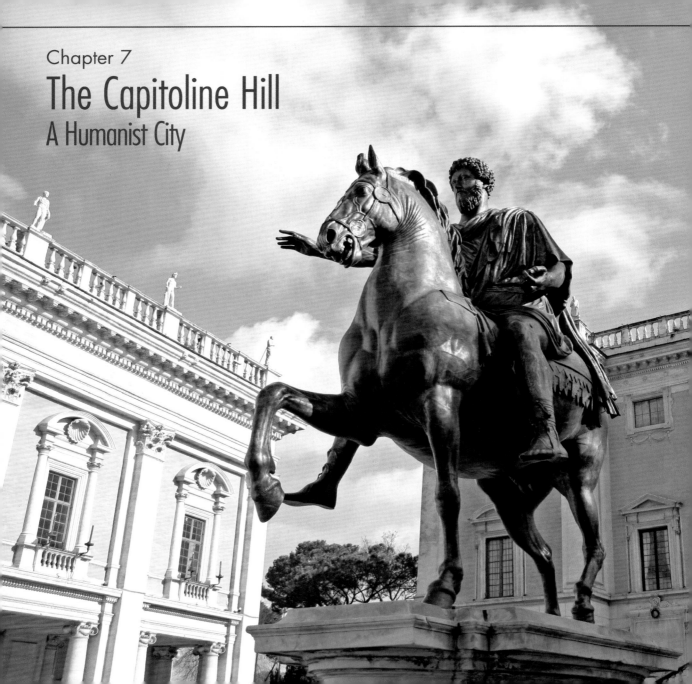

The Capitoline Hill
A Humanist City

On December 10, 1537, Michelangelo stood at the top of the Capitoline Hill, one of the seven hills of Rome, and was granted Roman citizenship in a ceremony full of pomp and grandeur. But the splendor could not disguise the grubbiness of the site. What had once been described as the "golden capitol" had degenerated over centuries into a muddy hilltop, difficult to climb and treacherous to descend. In 1538, Pope Paul III asked Michelangelo to redesign the Capitoline Hill, or Campidoglio, and make it glorious again.

When the papal conclave met in 1534 and elected Paul III, a Farnese pope with strong ties to Rome and big ideas for its renaissance, they chose a man who would become one of Michelangelo's greatest patrons. Paul III was determined to change the mood of Rome, which had not rebounded from the destruction inflicted by Emperor Charles V's troops seven years earlier. The coronation of Pope Paul III took on the flavor of a Roman emperor's coronation, marked by games, tournaments, and pageants. In 1536, he revived *carnivale*—a celebration leading up to Ash Wednesday and the holy season of Lent. And when Charles V (an ally of the Farnese family and thus now an ally of the papacy) announced he would visit the city, Paul III ordered that the streets be widened and straightened to better handle the crowds expected to turn out to see the man who had previously terrorized those same streets.

Not only was the new pope determined to create a more attractive, safer, and healthier city, he was also convinced that Michelangelo was the man to help him achieve that vision. During the fifteen years of

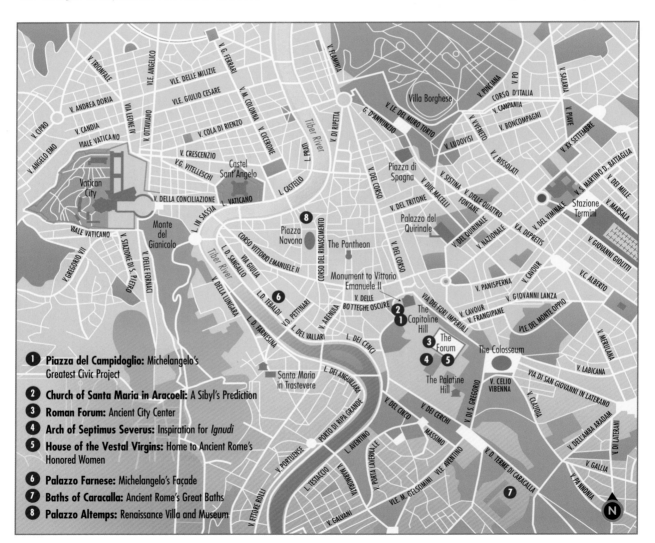

❶ **Piazza del Campidoglio:** Michelangelo's Greatest Civic Project

❷ **Church of Santa Maria in Aracoeli:** A Sibyl's Prediction

❸ **Roman Forum:** Ancient City Center

❹ **Arch of Septimus Severus:** Inspiration for *Ignudi*

❺ **House of the Vestal Virgins:** Home to Ancient Rome's Honored Women

❻ **Palazzo Farnese:** Michelangelo's Façade

❼ **Baths of Caracalla:** Ancient Rome's Great Baths

❽ **Palazzo Altemps:** Renaissance Villa and Museum

his papacy, Paul worked with Michelangelo to project papal power and live up to their shared humanist ideals through a series of civic projects. Paul's predecessors had revived Rome as *caput mundi*, but the Sack of Rome had undermined that status. Paul set out to remind the world that Rome was still the center of civilization. He did so by bringing the city back to its roots.

In ancient Rome, all roads literally led to the Capitoline Hill. It stood at the center of the city, and thus of the empire. During the Middle Ages, the hilltop became the site of public executions; by the Renaissance, what had once crowned an empire was now abandoned and swampy. When Charles V visited Rome in 1536, he tried to ascend the Capitoline Hill, but it was so muddy that he could not get to the top.

When Paul III approached Michelangelo to transform this morass, he was asking the artist to take on both a symbolic and a literal restoration. The project involved defining a safe and accessible entrance to the hill from the city, converting a muddy plateau into a level, paved area, and restoring the once grand structures that sat atop the hill. All this had to be done while respecting the existing buildings, including the church of Santa Maria in Aracoeli.

Michelangelo's plan called for an impressive program of construction that would reinforce Rome's position as a powerful city. Traditional Roman architects tamed large spaces by marking the center of the space and then designing in a radius around the center. For example, in the center of the Pantheon's floor is a circle upon which stood a ceremonial brazier where sacrifices were burned. The rest of the building radiates out from that central ceremonial spot. In similar fashion, Michelangelo began by placing a striking object—a statue of

Marcus Aurelius, the only equestiran bronze to have survived from the Roman Empire—at the center of the new piazza atop the Capitoline Hill and then designing outward along the piazza's radii.

The original bronze sculpture of Marcus Aurelius was removed from the piazza in 1981 because it was being corroded by the weather; it is now housed yards away in the Musei Capitolini. A full-scale replica stands on the base Michelangelo designed for the original.

Piazza del Campidoglio.

A Challenging Commission

In the ❶ **Piazza del Campidoglio**, Michelangelo faced a major challenge: the existing buildings. Now, as then, the Palazzo Senatorio and the Palazzo dei Conservatori sit close to each other, but they sit at odd angles, and the ancient church of Santa Maria in Aracoeli looks nothing like the other buildings. Charged with preserving both palazzi and the church, Michelangelo had to devise a means of relating them to each other as well as to the site as a whole. He found the perfect solution in the use of an oval, which allowed him to create a space of symmetry and grandeur from several disparate elements. He pulled everything together with a design that married the old and the new.

The Palazzo dei Conservatori, the seat of the elected city magistrate, featured a campanile (bell tower) that was off-center in relationship to the building supporting it. Michelangelo moved the campanile to the center of the palazzo. He then unified the two palazzi and gave the whole courtyard a sense of balance and rhythm by constructing wide pilasters (rectangular

supports that resemble flat columns) on both
buildings. Rather than letting the eye focus on
the many tiny windows and openings of the
building, the pilasters draw the eye up and
create a larger, less confusing pattern upon
which to focus. To further balance the
composition, Michelangelo designed a third
building (the Palazzo Nuovo) to mimic the
Palazzo dei Conservatori. Together, the three
buildings now house the Musei Capitolini as
well as Rome's city hall.

The Piazza del Campidoglio feels like an outdoor
room—a design element with which Renaissance
Italians were intimately familiar. Much of Italian
life takes place in outdoor rooms: the piazza is the
center of the neighborhood; the courtyard is the
center of a wealthy Italian's home. The Piazza
del Campidoglio became a place for outdoor
ceremonies—a role that it still plays. Today the
piazza is often filled with wedding parties; Rome's
city hall is one of only two places in the city (the
other is at the Baths of Caracalla) where a civil
ceremony can take place.

Michelangelo died before construction on the
Capitoline Hill was completed. His friend and
protégé Tommaso de' Cavalieri oversaw the
construction and preserved Michelangelo's
vision. One element of the final design—
Michelangelo's oval, star-patterned pavement—
was not installed until 1940, during the reign
of Benito Mussolini. It is ironic that Michelangelo's humanist vision of an elegant piazza
was completed centuries later by a fascist
dictator. Although Mussolini and Michelangelo
shared a respect for Italian history and a taste
for awe-inspiring architecture, Michelangelo was a
committed republican (he designed fortifications for

The Piazza del Campidoglio is often bustling with brides, grooms, and their
families. In Italy, unless a wedding ceremony is performed in a Catholic church,
the couple must also conduct a civil ceremony before their marriage is
considered legal.

the defense of Florence) and his architecture, unlike
Mussolini's demeanor, was neither overbearing nor
self-indulgent.

Humanism

The task of restoring a civic space infused with historic significance called for an architect knowledgeable about the arts as well as politics, science, and history. Michelangelo's humanist education and philosophy made him the perfect man for the job.

Humanists prized an education in the art and literature of ancient Greece and Rome; they believed that those schooled in the classics would become successful, cultured, and civilized and would use their education to help create a society that would be wisely governed, industrious, prosperous, and pious. Humanism began as an intellectual current among the elite, but it gradually flowed down through the social strata until humanist principles permeated Italian society. Humanist thinking transformed political life, military theory, science, commerce, poetry, and art. Education became de rigueur for women in some social circles; even among women of the lower classes, literacy became more important. The educated woman, however, was stuck. Her knowledge was an end in itself rather than a means to an end, because society frowned upon the idea of a woman working outside of the home.

Men faced no such restrictions. The consummate humanist was Leonardo da Vinci (1452–1519). Da Vinci the scientist analyzed human anatomy, designed flying machines, and invented a steam engine. Da Vinci the engineer prepared plans to build bridges, divert rivers, and besiege cities. Da Vinci the painter produced beautiful, precise canvases that are both distinctive and lyrical. Da Vinci the designer created costumes for theatrical productions and sets for elaborate court festivals.

The Roman Forum

In 1538, the view from the Capitoline Hill was expansive. Sixty-three-year-old Michelangelo could see his home at the foot of the hill and the sprawl of the city all around. But the view toward the Palatine Hill was shocking. Within Michelangelo's lifetime, and primarily at the direction of his papal patrons, the buildings in

Musei Capitolini

Pope Sixtus IV effectively founded the Musei Capitolini, the oldest public collection of ancient art, in 1471. The pontiff donated four works to the people of Rome, establishing a tradition that continued through the Renaissance as popes donated treasures long hidden within churches and palaces to the people of the city.

The donated art originally sat in the piazza, open to the elements and on public display. However, as the collection grew and conservators also began to purchase pieces, the art was moved into the Palazzo dei Conservatori, where pieces were arranged in the courtyard and rooms. The museum complex grew and expanded into all three buildings on the piazza and now extends through a subterranean space beneath Michelangelo's oval courtyard.

Santa Maria in Aracoeli

The ❷ church of Santa Maria in Aracoeli was more than just an obstacle for Michelangelo's construction project on the Capitoline Hill. It marked the spot where, according to legend, a Roman sibyl predicted the coming of Jesus Christ—a moment fusing Rome's pagan and Christian histories. The Renaissance traveler, looking beyond Santa Maria in Aracoeli, would have seen the convent attached to the church as well as numerous other minor buildings scattered down the hill, spilling out in the direction of Macel de' Corvi, where Michelangelo lived.

the area called the
❸ **Roman Forum** were
largely disassembled
and harvested for
construction material
and museum pieces,
leaving the skeletal
remains of an empire's
crossroads.

Ancient Rome was an
enormous city, and
the Roman Forum was
its center—the heart
of commerce, politics,
and religion. As with
the *place* of France
and the piazza of later
Italy, life in the city
revolved around the
Forum. Filled with
temples, palaces, and
civic buildings and
surrounded by market
areas, the Roman
Forum hummed and
pulsed.

The top of the Capitoline Hill offers an excellent view of the Roman Forum. The Arch of Septimus Severus is in the foreground; the Palatine Hill and palatial ruins lay in the background.

As the Roman
Empire declined,
however, so too did
the Roman Forum. Eventually, the Forum fell into
ruin, becoming known as the Campo Vaccino ("cow
pasture"), a popular spot for grazing both cattle and
sheep. Olive trees sprouted among the debris, and the
air smelled of sage, rosemary, and thyme.

Pope Julius II was one of many who pirated vast
quantities of building materials from the Forum. In his
zeal to rebuild Rome and exalt the papacy, Julius II
ignored the protests of Michelangelo and the painter
Raphael, among others, who were upset by the
wholesale destruction of the ruins. Workers hauled
away marble and metal at an amazing rate, dismantling
entire buildings in the space of a month. Ancient
marble slabs were ground down to limekiln dust, used
to make cement.

Raphael, appointed superintendent of antiquities in 1515, submitted a report to Pope Leo X:

> I behold this noble city, which was the queen of the world, so wretchedly wounded as to be almost a corpse. . . . The famous works which now more than ever should appear in the flower of their beauty were burned and destroyed by the brutal rage and savage passions of men wicked as the wild beasts.

Most of what survived the pillaging survived thanks to one of two circumstances: consecration as a church or burial over time. Built in 203 A.D., the ❹ **Arch of Septimus Severus** commemorates the victories of Septimus Severus against the Parthians. The arch was partly buried during Michelangelo's day, allowing him a close view of the figures at the top of the arch and deterring would-be plunderers. The east face of the arch bears figures that reappear as *ignudi* in the Sistine Chapel, and the arch itself served as a precedent for Julius II's tomb.

Museums and collectors spirited away most of the marble figures that once graced the Forum. A procession of female figures still lines the atrium of the ❺ **House of the Vestal Virgins,** however, hinting at the kind of decoration that adorned the Forum before it was buried in the sage and thistle of the Campo Vaccino.

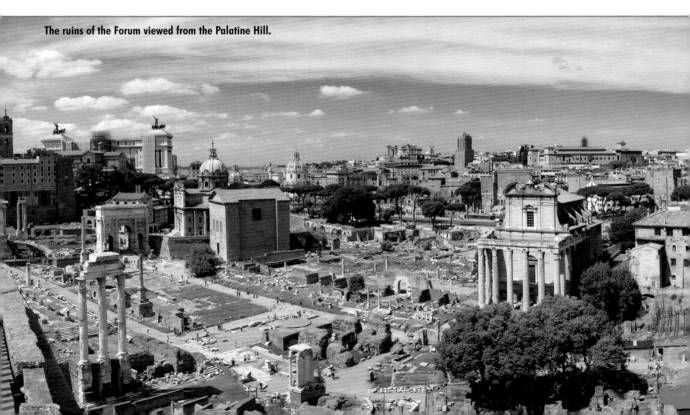

The ruins of the Forum viewed from the Palatine Hill.

Dedicated to the service of Vesta, the goddess of home and hearth, the Vestal Virgins held an elevated religious and social position. Selected between the ages of six and ten from among the daughters of Rome's patrician families, each of the six virgin priestesses served for thirty years. Thereafter, they could retire and marry, but few left their pampered, comfortable lives, in part because they considered it bad luck to do so.

The ruins of the virgins' home give a sense of the women's importance. Among Roman women, the virgins ranked second only to the empress and warranted deference from the entire empire. Their residence, located adjacent to the temple where they served, featured rose gardens, a pool, fountains, and a hall filled with memorials and honors bestowed upon them by thankful citizens. This complex in the crowded and expensive center of the Forum boasted fifty rooms on the ground floor alone, and there were probably two or three floors above. The virgins tended the sacred flame to Vesta, a symbol of the state, and enjoyed all kinds of preferential treatment, including special seats at the theater and the Colosseum. Their vows of chastity, however, were binding, and they faced a live burial in the "field of the wicked" (*campus sceleratus*) if they broke those vows.

The Vestal Virgins' lifestyle and social importance declined with the growth of Christianity; by the Renaissance, they had become the subjects of myth.

The Arch of Septimus Severus was once topped by bronze sculptures of a chariot drawn by six horses, but they have long since vanished.

Michelangelo on Titian

In 1545, Pope Paul III invited the Venetian artist Titian to Rome, where Michelangelo paid him a visit. As he entered Titian's studio, Michelangelo saw that Titian was at work on *Danaë*, a painting of a female figure from Greek mythology commissioned by Ottavio Farnese. He liked Titian's use of color but disliked his soft figures. Titian paid less attention than Michelangelo did to anatomy, and the Venetian's figures tended to be plump and round rather than muscular and taut. Michelangelo commented, "If Titian . . . had been assisted by art and design as greatly as he had been by Nature, especially in imitating live subjects, no artist could achieve better or paint better, for he possesses a splendid spirit and a most charming and lively style."

Nevertheless, Michelangelo drew upon their example when he painted the quartet of sibyls—powerful, spiritual women—on the ceiling of the Sistine Chapel.

A Palace for Paul III

Cardinal Alessandro Farnese had been orchestrating the construction of the ❻ **Palazzo Farnese** for seventeen years when he was elected pope in 1534. As Pope Paul III, he engaged Antonio da Sangallo to complete the building, making him the third architect to be involved with the project. The least gifted of Donato Bramante's students, Sangallo was the first Renaissance architect to be trained only in architecture and he devoted himself to his profession. He was the leading architect in Rome from 1520 to 1546. What he lacked as a designer, he made up for in his abilities as an engineer and builder; his designs lacked finesse (and his decorative schemes tended to be fussy, busy, and repetitive) but they have endured the wear and tear of centuries.

A palazzo such as the Farnese was designed primarily as an expression of power and strength, although it also functioned effectively as a comfortable residence. The business of running a large household took place on the ground floor, which contained offices and kitchens. Goods delivered to the palazzo courtyard could easily be unloaded and carried to the larders and storerooms that also occupied the ground floor.

What Italians refer to as the *primo piano* (the "first floor")—what Americans would call the second floor—existed to impress, for it was here that wealthy Italians of the Renaissance would entertain. Featuring reception halls and large spaces for public ceremonies decorated with grandiose designs and luxurious furnishings, the first floor showcased the family's wealth and standing. The primary family quarters also occupied this floor; lesser family

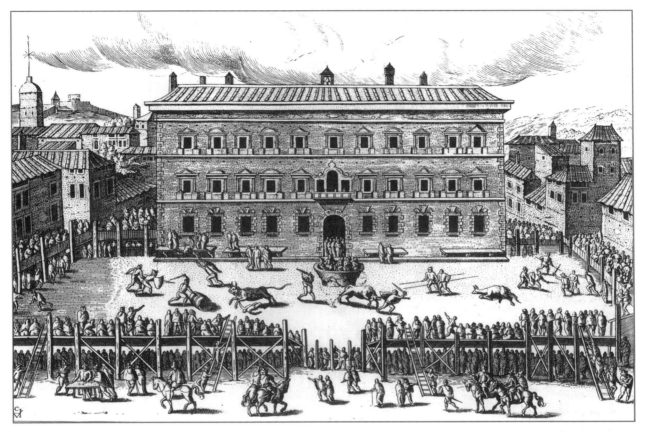

This drawing from the mid-1500s shows a bullfight in front of the Palazzo Farnese. Note the people in the tub; Michelangelo created fountains for the front of the palazzo using tubs from the Baths of Caracalla.

members and retainers lived on the floor above. Servants slept in the mezzanines between the floors or in attics.

The death of Sangallo in 1546 brought a halt to the Farnese project as well as to the construction of St. Peter's Basilica, a project Sangallo had inherited in 1539. Eventually, Michelangelo assumed responsibility

for both: he was commanded to take on the building of St. Peter's, and he won the Palazzo Farnese project in a design contest. By that time, the palazzo's façade was finished to the base of the third story. Following tradition, Sangallo's designs called for the third floor to diminish in scale compared to the first and second floors. Michelangelo's design did not follow suit. He raised the height of the third floor and submitted models for the heavy cornice that was later installed on that same floor. He also changed the central window design. These departures from classical dimensions raised eyebrows among Sangallo's devotees, for the third floor would now dominate the building design, even though, as the living quarters for lower-status family members, the third floor of a building usually received the least aesthetic consideration. In the end, Michelangelo's treatment of the third floor made the Palazzo Farnese the most distinctive and imposing building on the piazza.

Michelangelo's dreams for the Farnese were grand. In 1546, a sculpture of Hercules with a bull was discovered in the ❼ **Baths of Caracalla.** Inspired, the artist designed a fountain featuring the treasure for the front of the Farnese. He proposed extending the palace's grounds all the way to the river and across, uniting the Palazzo Farnese with the Villa Farnesina on the other side and creating a grand family estate with lush gardens and antiquities dotted throughout the grounds. The grander vision was never executed, however, and all that remains of Michelangelo's dream today is an arched walkway across Via Giulia.

In the piazza today sit two enormous fountains made from marble tubs. The tubs came from

Michelangelo's passageway over Via Giulia.

The Baths of Caracalla

Located not far from the Circus Maximus, the Baths of Caracalla were built by the Emperor Caracalla and dedicated in 216 A.D. Among the smaller of Rome's bathing complexes, the buildings could accommodate sixteen hundred bathers. The water ran from a specially constructed spur of the Aqua Marcia. They fell out of use after the Goths cut off the water supply in 537, but in their glory days, the baths were filled with fine statuary and mosaics, frescoed walls, a variety of bathing facilities, and a gymnasium. Baths functioned both as public meeting spaces and as places for entertainment. Emperors seeking to curry favor with the citizens of Rome often built baths—each complex outdoing the last—and many emperors opened the baths for free, though fees for bathing were never high, because bathing was highly regarded by the ancients.

During the sixteenth century, excavations of the Baths of Caracalla revealed numerous beautiful works of art, most of which ended up in the Farnese family collection. Today, the ruins attest to the scale of the Roman Empire's passion for bathing.

The tubs used in the fountains in front of the Palazzo Farnese came from the Baths of Caracalla.

the Baths of Caracalla and sport fleurs-de-lis—the Farnese family symbol—spouting water. The Palazzo Farnese now houses the French Embassy and is closed to the public, but the Piazza Farnese hums with activity and hosts several charming cafes with excellent views of Michelangelo's design. Just a block away, the bars and pizzerias of the Piazza di Campo dei Fiori are less dignified but make for a pleasant place to watch people shopping at the open-air flower market.

Palazzo Altemps

The Palazzo Farnese is closed to the public, but the ❶ **Palazzo Altemps** offers people the chance to visit a beautiful upper-class Renaissance residence. Frescoes grace the ceilings and walls of many of the rooms—especially in the public areas of the *primo piano*. The courtyard once provided a space for theatrical performances. Today, the Palazzo Altemps houses an impressive collection of ancient sculpture, including many pieces celebrated and imitated during the Renaissance.

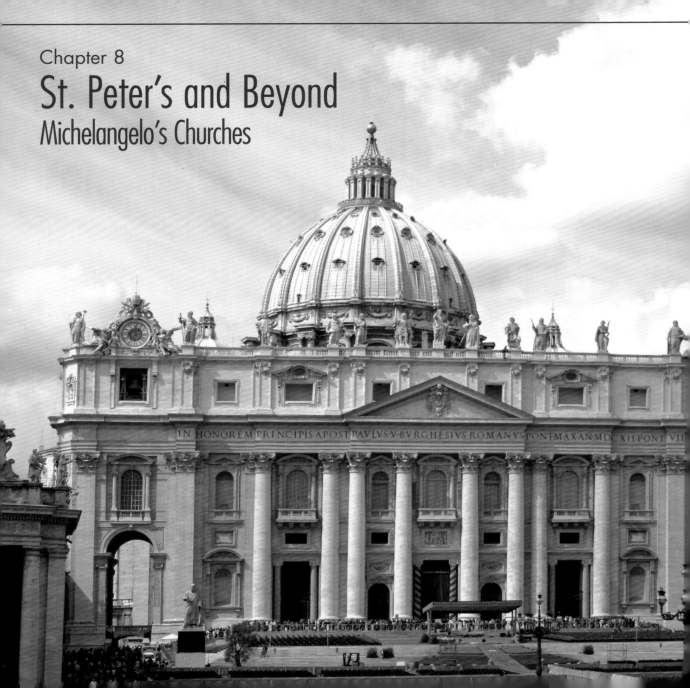

Chapter 8

St. Peter's and Beyond
Michelangelo's Churches

St. Peter's Basilica welcomes millions of visitors each year.

I call God to witness that I was set to building St. Peter's by Pope Paul ten years ago against my will and with the greatest pressure, . . . [but] if I abandoned it now, it would be nothing less than the greatest shame to lose all the reward of the labors I have endured for the love of God in the aforesaid ten years.

—Michelangelo, 1557

Michelangelo resisted getting involved with the St. Peter's Basilica project as long as possible, despite pressure from several popes and fellow artists. Enormous and expensive, construction of a new St. Peter's Basilica had been the obsession of every pope since 1506, when Julius II decided to replace the old St. Peter's so that his tomb, a monument designed by Michelangelo, would fit inside.

The original St. Peter's, a building Michelangelo liked and admired, sat on marshy ground in the Vatican—a spot chosen by Emperor Constantine. Julius II dreamed of replacing the fourth-century basilica with a building that would symbolize the very considerable power, wealth, and authority of the Renaissance church, knowing that he would not live to see its completion.

The new St. Peter's would forever change the scale and tone of ecclesiastical architecture. Yet the costs of building such an enormous structure would also contribute to the division of Western Christianity and an enduring reduction in papal power.

Ecclesiastical Architecture

Roman parish churches—today there are more than six hundred—played a variety of roles during the Renaissance. They offered a venue for the most important rituals of life: birth, first communion, marriage, and death. According to Catholic doctrine, the church in all its guises (e.g., clerics, buildings, and ceremonies) functioned as the "earthly manifestation of Christ's incarnation" and mediated between God and

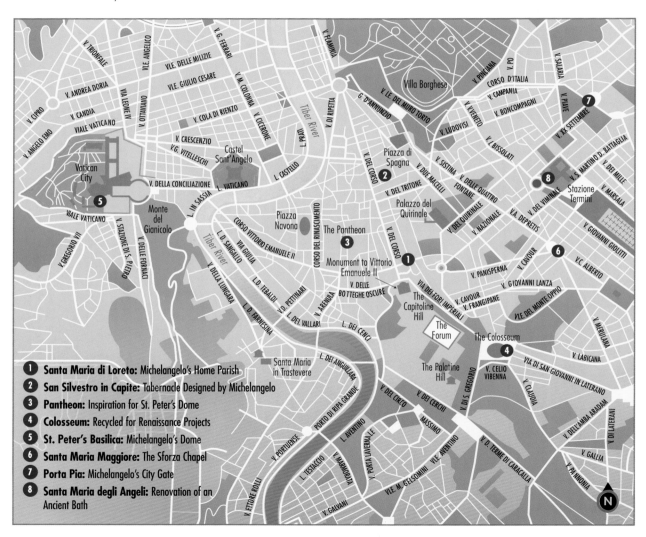

1. **Santa Maria di Loreto:** Michelangelo's Home Parish
2. **San Silvestro in Capite:** Tabernacle Designed by Michelangelo
3. **Pantheon:** Inspiration for St. Peter's Dome
4. **Colosseum:** Recycled for Renaissance Projects
5. **St. Peter's Basilica:** Michelangelo's Dome
6. **Santa Maria Maggiore:** The Sforza Chapel
7. **Porta Pia:** Michelangelo's City Gate
8. **Santa Maria degli Angeli:** Renovation of an Ancient Bath

the people; without the church, people could have no contact with God.

In an uneducated and illiterate society, parish churches also offered entertainment. With holy water and the Eucharist, saints and their relics, paintings and sculptures, and a calendar full of colorful festivals, churches provided congregants with the pomp, ceremony, and spectacle their daily lives usually lacked.

While living in the neighborhood of Macel de' Corvi, Michelangelo probably worshipped at the parish church of ❶ **Santa Maria di Loreto,** which adjoined the small courtyard his house faced. Small but impressive, the church was built in the early sixteenth century by Antonio da Sangallo the elder. The dome was added later, in 1573, by Jacopo del Duca, a devotee of Michelangelo.

The daily experience at mass in the 1500s was not necessarily one of pious reverence. Most of the service was conducted in Latin, a language spoken only by the educated elite, so most members of the congregation were left to their own devices. During sermons, which could stretch for hours, congregants behaved much as they would on the street: knitting, begging, spitting, joking, heckling, swearing, sleeping—even firing guns.

Physically, churches stood in the middle of their communities. Most neighborhood churches opened up onto a piazza. During festivals and pageants to celebrate saints and martyrs, politicians campaigned, merchants hawked their wares, and vendors sold all

kinds of food. In Renaissance Italy, the sacred life could not be separated from the secular.

This was true in part because Christian architecture had grown from secular roots. Until the fourth century,

Santa Maria di Loreto was just steps away from Michelangelo's home. The church's dome was inspired by the dome that Michelangelo designed for St. Peter's.

Christians had been forced to gather in private, sometimes secret, places to worship. When Constantine announced his conversion to Christianity, he began to build sacred spaces and constructed three impressive churches in Rome: San Giovanni in Laterano, San Pietro in Vaticano (St. Peter's), and San Paolo fuori le Mura. But the larger Christian community did not have the kind of money that Constantine did to build churches. Thus, they continued the Roman tradition of reusing materials when creating their sacred spaces. They recycled something else, too: the architecture of Roman basilicas.

The basilica, constructed in the center of a city as a place to conduct business transactions, anchored the ancient Roman economy. All basilicas have the same basic proportions, being twice as long as they are wide. They also adhere to roughly the same internal design, with rows of columns forming aisles and delineating smaller areas to each side. The Christian church adopted this basic floor plan—sometimes even turning ancient basilicas into churches. Shops in ancient structures became side chapels and altars in Christian buildings. Thus, the construction techniques of ancient Rome became the standard for Christian construction, and the basilica became the foundation of Christian architecture. There are now thirty-one basilican churches in Rome alone.

The Pantheon

Michelangelo based his designs for St. Peter's dome on two sources of inspiration. One was a church in which he had played and studied as a boy: Santa Maria del Fiore in Florence. Florence's Duomo was the first dome built after the fall of the Roman Empire; designed by Filippo Brunelleschi, the dome was completed in 1436. Michelangelo's other inspiration was in Rome and was considerably older: the ❸ **Pantheon.**

Although not a basilica, the single most aesthetically powerful building of ancient Rome was the Pantheon. Michelangelo, an ardent admirer of the Pantheon, attributed its power to *disegno angelico e non umano* (angelic and not human design). It was consecrated in the seventh century as a Christian church, Santa Maria Rotunda, but the building remains better known the world over by its pagan name.

Since 25 B.C., and perhaps before, the site on which the Pantheon stands has been sacred. Agrippa, a statesman and general in the first century B.C., erected a rectangular pantheon (literally, a place of worship honoring all gods) on the site. However, Agrippa's structure burned down—twice.

Christian Relics

During the Roman Empire, Christians often established communities of faith—and later built churches—in locations where saints and martyrs had died or were buried. The remains of these venerated figures came to represent a conduit between the living and God and served as a reminder of the believer's task in life. Churches competed ardently for relics, either homegrown or imported, because crowds were drawn to relics. And crowds of pilgrims and locals conferred fame and status on a church as well as on its clergy.

Roman churches boast a wide range of relics. Although many of the most cherished are held at the Vatican—according to tradition, the remains of St. Peter himself rest underneath the altar in St. Peter's Basilica—other churches also possess significant relics. ❷ **San Silvestro in Capite**, with an altar designed by Michelangelo, houses what is claimed to be the head of St. John the Baptist as well as the face of Christ on a veil. Santa Maria degli Angeli contains a chapel of relics where the remains of martyrs associated with the Baths of Diocletian are housed. Santa Maria Maggiore has the crib of the Christ Child, and San Paolo alle Tre Fontane sits on three springs that, according to tradition, emerged when Paul was beheaded at the site.

Emperor Hadrian erected a replacement that was dedicated in 126 A.D. He inspired centuries of confusion by putting this inscription on his new building: M•Agrippa•L•F•Cos•Tertium•Fecit. Translated, it reads, "Marcus Agrippa, the son of Lucius, three times consul, built this." (Hadrian, in a rather un-emperor-like fashion, often neglected to put his own name on buildings he constructed.) Thus, for centuries the Pantheon was thought by many to be two hundred years older than it actually is. The bricks used in the building's construction, however, reveal the truth. They bear stamps dated to Hadrian's reign.

In 609, Pope Boniface IV consecrated the Pantheon as a Christian church "after the pagan filth was removed." That "pagan filth" included sculptures of Mars, Venus, and a deified Julius Caesar as well as caryatids—draped female figures that functioned as columns and bronze figures on the pediment over the porch.

Even after the building's consecration, Romans did not hesitate to alter their greatest relic. In 663, Emperor Constans II melted down the gilded bronze roof tiles, which had reflected the sun's radiance. Pope Pius IV restored the bronze pilasters at the entrance but had the original doors gold plated. Despite all the plundering, the Pantheon was ultimately saved thanks to its consecration. Of all the ancient structures in Rome, it is the best preserved.

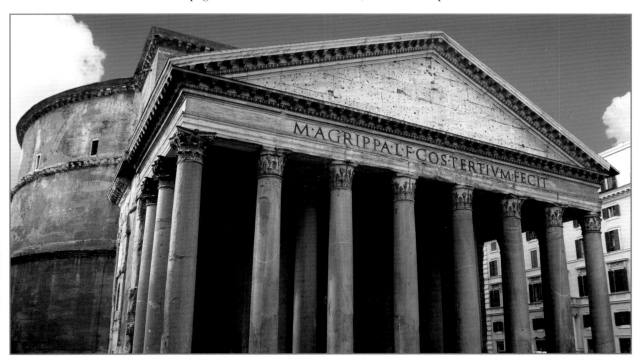

The Pantheon has been in continuous use—as a temple, a church, and a tomb—since its construction nearly two thousand years ago.

117

The Pantheon has remained a symbol of the beauty and accomplishments not just of Rome but of Italy as a whole. When Raphael died in 1520, he was buried in the rotunda, in the building he admired most. Vittorio Emanuele II, the first king of a united Italy, was also buried in the Pantheon, his internment signifying the sacred, historical, and political continuity of the country.

An Impressive Inspiration

The two most distinctive elements of the Pantheon are its dome and its oculus. For the ancient Roman worshipper, the oculus (a circular hole in the roof) connected the world of the gods with the human world. The sun, the eye of Zeus, peered through the oculus, tracking light across the floor and marking the days and the passing of the year. The gods, Roman cosmology, and the emperor were all intimately linked, and the Pantheon embodied that link.

But it is the Pantheon's dome that has always most impressed visitors. A symbol of permanence and divinity, the dome has been associated with sacred architecture since its construction. The dome uses a compression system of buttresses to carry the weight of five thousand tons of concrete. The concrete itself was delicately engineered to be progressively lighter as the poured panels came closer and closer to the oculus.

As Renaissance artists and architects looked to the ruins of ancient Rome for instruction and inspiration, they tried to divine—and then to copy—the mathematical formulas that their predecessors had employed to construct such marvels. But even many of the simplest techniques known to the ancients had been lost in the intervening centuries and remained hidden from view. The recipe for concrete, for example, had been lost, and Brunelleschi was left to construct his dome in Florence out of bricks and mortar.

The sun shines through the oculus of the Pantheon.

Unlike many of his colleagues, Michelangelo did not seek a mathematical solution to architecture, and instead adopted a more anthropomorphic approach. In studying buildings like the Pantheon, he looked at the interactions between the buildings and the people who occupied them. "It is certain," Michelangelo wrote, "that architectural members depend on the same rules as those governing the limbs of men." He attributed the design of the Pantheon to "angelic" design not because it followed particular rules, but because it inspired a particular emotion and exemplified a relationship between the human figure and the building itself—a relationship he would try to re-create in his design for St. Peter's Basilica.

The Colosseum

The ❹ Colosseum dominated Rome—until the new St. Peter's began to soar across the river. Emperor Titus inaugurated the Colosseum as a place of public entertainment in 80 A.D. Built to hold fifty thousand spectators, the Colosseum was intended as a place of public entertainment and gathering. It enjoyed nearly four centuries of use, beginning with one hundred days of games held at its opening.

On the first day of games in the Colosseum, five thousand animals were slaughtered in a riot of brutality and bloodlust. Although stories of Christians being fed to the lions in the Colosseum are fiction (those kinds of events happened at the Circus Maximus and elsewhere), the Colosseum did regularly host bloody gladiatorial battles. The floor of the arena was covered in sand to absorb blood, and underneath the floor a network of tunnels and rooms hid animals and people waiting to appear. The floor could even be flooded with water for mock marine battles. While the games were being played, spectators sat in relative comfort. Seats were assigned, and spectators ate and drank as they watched the events on the arena floor. A system of canvas shades at the top of the building kept the sun at bay.

Eventually, however, the Colosseum was abandoned. It was stripped of its metal fittings, and much of its stone ornamentation and decoration was reused in other building projects, including the Barberini and Canalleria palaces, the Ponte Sisto, and St. Peter's Basilica.

The best seats in the Colosseum were reserved for the emperor, his guests, and the Vestal Virgins, but tickets were inexpensive—and sometimes free—so that everyone could enjoy the entertainment. Note the now-exposed passages that were under the arena floor.

A Skillful Architect

When Donato Bramante (1444–1514) moved to Rome in 1499, he was already a well-established architect in other parts of Italy. Born near Urbino, Bramante had trained as a painter and, like most other artists of the Renaissance, had been educated in various media, including architecture. His work in Rome would transform and define the architectural styles of an entire generation.

After Michelangelo suggested to Julius II that the roof of St. Peter's would need to be raised to encompass the pope's tomb, Julius decided that a new church might be a better idea. He held a design contest to choose the architect, and Bramante won. In 1506, while Michelangelo was in Carrara choosing marble for the pope's tomb, the foundation was laid for the new St. Peter's Basilica.

From the start, the construction project was enormously expensive and time-consuming. Initially, there was some confusion as to whether the old church was to be remodeled or demolished. In 1512, Julius II issued a papal bull promising the completion of the new St. Peter's, and the remnants of the old church were destroyed.

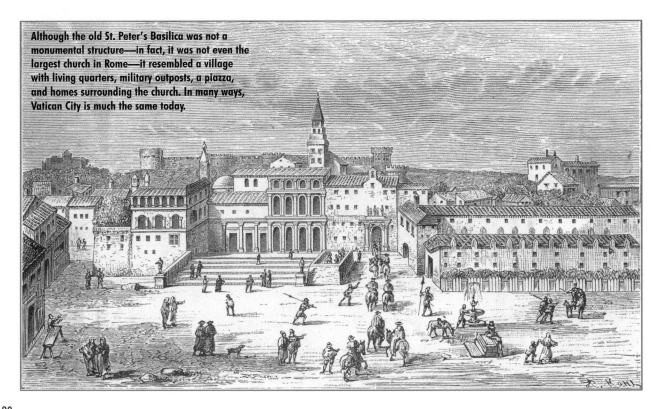

Although the old St. Peter's Basilica was not a monumental structure—in fact, it was not even the largest church in Rome—it resembled a village with living quarters, military outposts, a piazza, and homes surrounding the church. In many ways, Vatican City is much the same today.

While Michelangelo was at work in the Sistine Chapel, the destruction he saw across the way disturbed him greatly. He approached the pope, expressing his disapproval of Bramante's ruinous tendencies. Where Michelangelo would have carefully saved columns and capitals, Bramante (nicknamed "Maestro Ruinate") had simply and violently pulled them down. After Bramante's death, a satire was written that depicted him in heaven: the architect wanted to demolish everything there and build a new and better one—with access roads.

When Bramante began construction on the basilica, he started at the center of the building—the altar— and worked outward in concentric circles. Given that construction would take centuries, this approach would ensure that the building would grow uniformly from the core out. Beginning with four central piers and four buttressing arms, Bramante slowly began to raise a new building.

In 1514, at the age of seventy, Bramante died—just as the project was starting construction. Raphael, who had worked under Bramante's tutelage, was the logical replacement. But Raphael died just six years later, and in his wake came a succession of architects—each a little more removed from Bramante and his vision. Michelangelo watched from afar as the building took shape, never wishing to be involved with such a mammoth task.

Michelangelo and St. Peter's

Construction on the new ❺ **St. Peter's** continued for decades while Michelangelo worked on other commissions in Florence and then again in Rome. When Antonio da Sangallo the Younger, the latest in a succession of architects of St. Peter's, died in 1546, Pope Paul III chose Michelangelo to replace Sangallo.

Michelangelo accepted the job reluctantly. He knew he could do it—and do a better job than Sangallo. But ultimately he accepted the commission because he saw it as another opportunity to use his gifts to glorify God.

Michelangelo knew that wresting authority away from Sangallo's followers would be a battle, as it was proving with the Palazzo Farnese, another of Sangallo's projects. In order to defuse some of the opposition to his appointment—and to preserve a measure of independence from the papacy—he refused the usual compensation. This arrangement also allowed him to continue to work on the Palazzo Farnese, the Campidoglio, and other projects as they came up. He did acquire a contract, however, giving him all of the ferry tolls taken on the river at Piacenza.

The Church That Provoked a Revolution

In March 1517, Pope Leo X issued an order to sell indulgences in order to finance the continued construction of St. Peter's. An indulgence excused a sinner from doing penance for sins committed. Because the church needed money, Leo X allowed the sale of indulgences in advance. In other words, people could pay for sins they had not yet committed.

Martin Luther, who had been shocked by Rome's poverty and immorality when he visited in 1510, was so outraged by Leo X's decision that he publicly protested, nailing a litany of complaints about the Catholic Church and a program of reforms to the door of his parish church in Wittenberg, Germany. One of Luther's primary concerns was the construction of St. Peter's. "Why does not the pope whose wealth is today greater than the riches of the richest build just this one church of St. Peter with his own money, rather than with the money of poor believers?"

The Reformation had begun.

"Upon This Rock I Will Build My Church"

Scholars and theologians have contemplated the question of St. Peter's final resting place for centuries. The Gospels never refer to Peter's martyrdom or his presence in Rome. Rome has claimed to house St. Peter's remains since the first century A.D., however, and the Catholic Church has always regarded him as the first pope, for Jesus proclaimed of him, "Upon this rock I will build my church." The inscription around the drum of Michelangelo's dome recites these words in six-foot-tall letters.

Peter is generally believed to have died at the hands of Nero in a massacre of Christians, who were treated as scapegoats for the fire that destroyed much of Rome in 64 A.D. On the site later occupied by the Vatican stood a circus (a track for chariot races and other amusements) where Nero tortured and killed his prey.

According to tradition, Peter was buried in a nearby necropolis. When Constantine built the first St. Peter's, he filled in the necropolis to create a solid foundation for his new basilica. That church, in turn, was demolished to make way for the new St. Peter's.

The hill on which the Vatican stands has long been a sacred place. The Etruscans celebrated rituals

The interior of the dome over St. Peter's is covered in mosaics and gold designed by Cavaliere d'Arpino in the seventeenth century. The lettering on the drum of the dome translates as, "You are Peter and upon this rock I will build my church."

there between 700 and 500 B.C. The ancient Romans built myriad temples on the hill, named for the "vates," or holy seers, who interpreted the moans and groans of the gassy, snake-infested swamp. When the old St. Peter's was destroyed, workers whispered about the "curse of St. Peter" and were terrified to unearth ancient, pagan relics during the laying of the new foundation. The terrorized workers thought the pagan relics were cursed.

In the mid-twentieth century, Pope Pius XII (1939–58) secretly authorized excavations underneath the altar in St. Peter's in hopes that Peter's remains might be identified. For ten years archaeologists labored covertly; they announced their findings in 1951. They had found St. Peter's tomb. Decades of bitter academic controversy ensued, with scholars ridiculing the archaeologists' methods and discoveries, while the archaeologists fought among themselves publicly.

Do the altar of St. Peter's and Michelangelo's dome sit atop the remains of St. Peter? During the papacy of John Paul II (1978–2005), tours of the *scavi* (excavations) made no mention of St. Peter. However, under Pope Benedict XVI, archaeologists claiming to have unearthed the saint's remains have found a more sympathetic ear.

So, although to most people it looked like he was not being paid for his work at St. Peter's, he was in fact making money.

Michelangelo had been partial to the old St. Peter's, but he recognized the value and beauty in Bramante's plan. About Sangallo's design, he wrote:

> The circle he puts outside cuts off all the light from Bramante's plan, and not only this, it has no light itself, and so many dark hiding places between the upper and lower parts that it is arranged conveniently for an infinity of mischief, such as hiding outlaws, coining false money, getting nuns with child and other mischief, such that when, in the evening, the aforesaid church would be locked, it would take twenty-five men to hunt out whoever might be lying hidden inside, and finding them would be hard for them.

Michelangelo contended that if Sangallo's design were to be implemented, the Pauline and Sistine chapels—among other buildings—would need to be destroyed. He had just completed frescoes in both chapels, so he had a considerable stake in seeing them preserved. Neither Michelangelo nor Sangallo's disciples would back down until finally the pope intervened, giving Michelangelo complete control over both the design and the people working on the project.

A Change in Plans

Bramante's design, a cross inscribed in a square with a dome like that over the Pantheon, reflected the Renaissance architect's interest in fundamental shapes and proportions. But his original design was diluted by subsequent architects. Sangallo in particular added fussy and uninspired designs to the building, completely losing Bramante's sense of style. By the time Michelangelo came to the project, he faced a partially constructed building lacking cohesion. Michelangelo returned to Bramante's original design. He wanted to keep the inner ring where Bramante had begun construction, but he peeled back the layers Sangallo had added. As with the Palazzo Farnese, Michelangelo unified the plan. He stripped the structure down to the original cross-and-square design, then set about installing the dome.

Bramante had designed a dome much like that of the Pantheon: a hemisphere inscribed into the cube of the building. Michelangelo recognized the engineering impossibility in the design: Bramante's dome was simply too flat to be self-supporting using the construction techniques of the day. In 1547, Michelangelo sent a letter to his nephew Lionardo requesting the measurements for the dome Brunelleschi had constructed in 1436 on the Duomo in Florence.

Working with clay models, Michelangelo changed his design as the building rose. He worked with the space in the same way that he worked with stone, shaping the interior space of the church rather than prescribing the container around it. In his mind, the building was a container for a space rather than an end in itself. He changed the type of stone he planned to use and the size of architectural elements as he saw the space grow.

Although Michelangelo produced models for various elements of St. Peter's, he kept the overall plan for St. Peter's a secret, even from his friends. But his advocates realized that the architect would not live forever, and in the interest of preserving his vision, they begged him to produce a full model. Michelangelo resisted for several reasons. To do so would be, in part, to acknowledge his own mortality. In addition, it would also commit him to a design that could not easily be changed.

Finally, in 1548, he relented. He knew that the construction of St. Peter's would take centuries. He wanted to accomplish enough within his lifetime that his vision for the building could not be changed—setting the construction down a path that could not be reversed. The model, which began with clay studies, took three years to construct.

In 1549, when Michelangelo was eighty-four, Giovan Francesco Lottini, a papal insider, wrote, "Michelangelo Buonarroti is in fact so old that even if he wished he could not move more than a few miles, and for some time now goes little or rarely to St. Peter's. Other than which,

Family Pressures

By the time he started work on St. Peter's, Michelangelo was in his seventies and suffering from kidney stones. His age and illness did not prevent him from continuing a lifelong occupation, however: corresponding with his family.

Among those to whom he wrote was his nephew Lionardo, a flighty young man who lived in Florence and stood to inherit much of the childless Michelangelo's fortune. In 1550, Michelangelo sent a letter to Lionardo acknowledging a gift of wine the young man had sent and asking that he send along some papers from Florence. "On the matter of [your] getting married," Michelangelo wrote, "there is no more talk, and everyone tells me I should give you a wife, as if I had a thousand in a sack. I have no way to give thought to it, because I have no knowledge of the citizens. I should be very glad if you were to find one, and you must, but I can do nothing more."

Michelangelo patiently explained to his family, time and again, that he was too busy in Rome to return to Florence. Yet his family continued to lure him home with gifts of pears, cheeses, and other Florentine goods that Michelangelo missed.

the model will need many months to complete it, and he is under the obligation, and the desire, to finish it."

Scholars argue over the degree of Michelangelo's influence on St. Peter's as it exists today, but no one can dispute that his design gave a solid center to a building process that was floundering and that those who came after him respected his work. The dome that soars over Rome today is largely as the artist envisioned it. However, the portico he designed for the front—resembling the Pantheon—was never constructed. Instead, Carlo Maderno (1556–1629) lengthened the nave to form a Latin cross and added the façade. The interior reflects the contributions of seventeenth-century architects and a shift from the classical designs of the High

Changing Plans

Each architect who worked on St. Peter's modified the plans. Bramante's original Greek cross was relatively simple and open, though very large. As construction began, his plans evolved to include more structural support as he anticipated the weight of a dome overhead. Sangallo's design for an elaborate Latin cross created many small, isolated spaces within the large church. When Michelangelo took over the project, he destroyed much of the construction done under Sangallo. His design, the simplest of all, created large, open spaces for worship surrounded by massive piers and walls to support the enormous dome overhead.

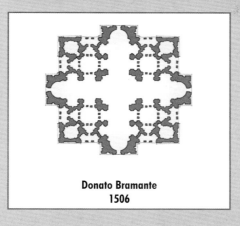

Donato Bramante
1506

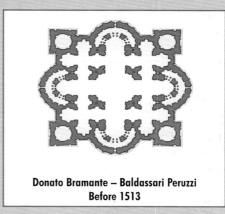

Donato Bramante – Baldassari Peruzzi
Before 1513

Antonio da Sangallo
1539

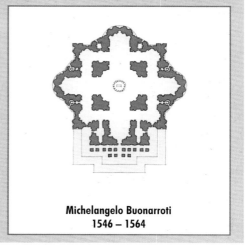

Michelangelo Buonarroti
1546 – 1564

Bernini's *Baldacchino*

In 1623, as work on St. Peter's neared completion, Pope Urban VIII commissioned a *baldacchino*, a canopy for the altar. Bernini's design was the only one submitted that was appropriate for the scale of Michelangelo's dome, under which it was to sit. Completed in 1633, the gilded *baldacchino* rises nearly one hundred feet in the air and is constructed of a thousand tons of bronze—decorations from the Pantheon melted down.

With a 100-foot-tall *baldacchino*, 450-foot-tall dome, seven-foot-tall cherubs, six-foot-tall letters, and figures of saints that are almost twenty feet tall, everything in St. Peter's is on a large scale.

Renaissance to the Baroque. After all, the nave was constructed a century after its foundation was laid—which allowed plenty of time for an evolution in taste.

Gian Lorenzo Bernini (1598–1680), a Baroque-era sculptor, architect, and painter, shaped the exterior of St. Peter's, defining the piazza in front. A double colonnade of 284 columns delineates Piazza San Pietro and welcomes visitors to the Vatican. In the words of the nineteenth-century English poet Robert Browning, "Columns in the colonnade / With arms wide open to embrace / The entry of the human race."

Michelangelo's Last Patron

When Pius IV was elected in 1559, Michelangelo was eighty-five and still supervising the construction of the Campidoglio and St. Peter's from his home at Macel de' Corvi. He would send notes up to the Vatican with a variety of instructions and comments. One note, for instance, complained, "You are aware I told Balduccio that he should not send his lime if it wasn't good. Now having sent poor stuff, which must be taken back without any question, one may believe that he had made an agreement with whoever accepted it."

Under Pius IV, the aging architect took on three more projects: a chapel at Santa Maria Maggiore, the Porta Pia, and the design of Santa Maria degli Angeli.

The church at ❻ **Santa Maria Maggiore** dates to the fifth century, though the building has changed much

over the years. In 1560, Michelangelo designed a small, oval-shaped chapel for the Sforza family; it was constructed after his death. It is now used for midday worship services and offers a simple, light space for meditation in the midst of an enormous structure bustling with tourists and pilgrims.

In March 1561, Pius IV asked Michelangelo to design a new gate for the city. Michelangelo presented him with

Piazza San Pietro features two large fountains as well as an ancient Egyptian obelisk brought to the city when the Romans conquered Egypt. Visitors can take an elevator to the roof level of St. Peter's and then climb 320 steps inside the shell of the dome to reach the top—and the best view of Rome in the city.

127

Snow in Summer

According to legend, the Virgin Mary appeared to Pope Liberius in a dream on August 4, 352, telling him to build a church on the Esquiline Hill. She said he would awake to snow on the hill outlining the design. The first church on the site of the Santa Maria Maggiore was called Santa Maria della Neve ("of the snow"). Each year on August 5, the church brings out snowmaking machines to celebrate the miraculous snowfall, attracting children from all over the city in the heat of the summer.

three separate designs, and the pope chose the least expensive. The ❼ **Porta Pia** was not part of the city's defenses: it faced into the city rather than away, standing as a purely ornamental reminder to those departing that they were leaving the sanctity and protection of Rome.

Constructed between 1561 and 1565, the gate was left unfinished after Pius IV's death. In the nineteenth

century, it was damaged by lightning and reconstructed. The top story, designed by Virginio Vespignani, was added in 1853 during reconstruction. Today, the Porta Pia houses the Museo Storico dei Bersaglieri, a museum of military history.

Pius IV also wanted a large, impressive church along Via Pia, near Michelangelo's Porta Pia. He approached Michelangelo about designing one. In an unusual move, the artist ended up transforming a room in the Baths of Diocletian, an ancient public bathing complex that had fallen into ruins, into a church.

As a humanist, Michelangelo respected the ancient ruins that dotted Rome. He was practical, though, and wanted to save money, for the pope's coffers were not as full as they once had been. Today, ❽ **Santa Maria degli Angeli** hardly resembles Michelangelo's original design. In the eighteenth century, architect Luigi Vanvitelli remodeled the church, moving the altar and adorning the walls with elaborate decorative elements. But the simplicity that Michelangelo desired exists—especially on the building's exterior, which maintains the look of a Roman ruin.

Working on architectural projects using advisors in the field to supervise the progress gave Michelangelo welcome reason to spend most of his time at home; but, though he was in failing health and reluctant to travel, his commitment to his art did not diminish. As he told Lionardo in a letter in 1557, "As for how I am, I am ill in body, with all the ills that the old usually have . . . for if I left the comforts for my troubles that I have here, I wouldn't have three days to live, and yet I do not . . . nor would I want to fail the construction of St. Peter's here, nor fail myself."

The Porta Pia.

The Baths of Diocletian

Between 298 and 306 A.D., Emperor Diocletian built the largest baths in ancient Rome. Covering more than thirty acres, the baths were a place not only for bathing and gossiping but also for sporting activities and public lectures. A trip to the *thermae* was an important part of daily life for the ancient Roman, and access to the baths was generally inexpensive or free.

Roman bathing complexes consisted of a variety of rooms, most named for the temperature of the water provided there. The *calidarium* offered patrons a hot bath; the *tepidarium* was a warm room for lounging; and the *frigidarium* gave visitors the chance to cool down. The *piscine* contained a swimming pool. Attendants and slaves staffed each room, pampering guests with oils, massages, shaves, and personal attention. Roman baths typically featured an elegant array of public artworks: frescoes, statues, fountains, and mosaics.

During the Renaissance, artists visited the disused Baths of Diocletian to study the decorative schemes on the walls, while treasure hunters came to unearth statuary and cart it off to private collections. Today, much of the Diocletian bathing complex lies in ruin or has disappeared entirely. Some pieces have been preserved, however, albeit in adapted form. Michelangelo transformed the *frigidarium* into Santa Maria degli Angeli, for example. What remains of the baths, beyond the church, today houses a museum.

Santa Maria degli Angeli has changed greatly since Michelangelo designed it, but it does retain the look of a Roman ruin, which was his intention.

Vasari published his biography in 1550. It included the life story not just of Michelangelo but of many other noted artists of his age. *Lives of the Painters, Sculptors, and Architects* more or less invented the genre of art history. With a focus on the artists of Florence, *Lives* shaped perceptions of good and great art for centuries, and Vasari held Michelangelo up as the supreme artist in his pantheon.

Michelangelo was not entirely pleased with Vasari's *Lives*, however. Vasari relied on others to recount Michelangelo's life rather than conversing directly

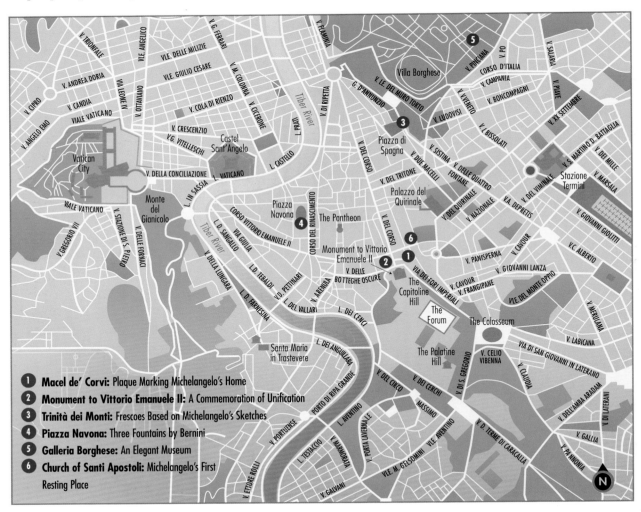

1. **Macel de' Corvi:** Plaque Marking Michelangelo's Home
2. **Monument to Vittorio Emanuele II:** A Commemoration of Unification
3. **Trinità dei Monti:** Frescoes Based on Michelangelo's Sketches
4. **Piazza Navona:** Three Fountains by Bernini
5. **Galleria Borghese:** An Elegant Museum
6. **Church of Santi Apostoli:** Michelangelo's First Resting Place

with Michelangelo, and his first edition presented false or flimsy accounts of important events in Michelangelo's life. For example, Vasari summarized Michelangelo's forty-year struggle with Julius II's tomb in one sentence. Michelangelo was offended and sent him a sonnet in response:

If you had with your pen or with your color
Given nature an equal in your art,
And indeed cut her glory down in part,
Handing us back her beauty lovelier,

You now, however, with a worthier labor,
Have settled down with learned hand to write,
And steal her glory's one remaining part
That you still lacked, by giving life to others.

Rivals she had in any century
In making beautiful works, at least would bow;
At their appointed ends they must arrive.

But you make their extinguished memory
Return blazing, and themselves, and you,
In spite of her eternally alive.

Although the poem appears to be complimentary, it is actually a cutting critique. Michelangelo, who thought Vasari lacked artistic talent, points out that Vasari is a better writer than painter. Moreover, as a humanist, Michelangelo believed that no one could replicate the natural world accurately. So the fame that he seems to write about at the end is actually infamy: Vasari would live on in shame. But Michelangelo's harshest criticism of Vasari came in another form: he commissioned a biography by Ascanio Condivi.

Condivi's *The Life of Michelangelo* appeared in 1553. Whereas Vasari's volume is

impersonal and inaccurate, Condivi's is warm and authoritative. Condivi had the confidence of Michelangelo and spent much time interviewing him. As a consequence, Condivi's account is more reliable than Vasari's—which explains why, when Vasari

This bust of Michelangelo by Vasari is part of Michelangelo's tomb in Florence.

133

revised *Lives*, he did so with a copy of Condivi's book in hand.

Curiously, Condivi disappeared from Michelangelo's circle of friends after the publication of his work, whereas Michelangelo and Vasari maintained a relationship until Michelangelo's death. Despite the criticism Michelangelo levied against him, Vasari was eager to please Michelangelo, revising *Lives* to portray Michelangelo's life in a more realistic light.

Family and Friends

Despite his advancing years, Michelangelo maintained close ties with his family in Florence, especially his favorite brother, Buonarroto. The artist often wrote Buonarroto with complaints about his life in Rome. Buonarroto once replied: "You must value your person more than a column, the whole quarry, the pope, and all the world . . . come home by all means and let everything else go to hell." When Buonarroto died in 1528, he left a daughter, Francesca, and a son, Lionardo, who became Michelangelo's only heir.

The Grieving Son
Upon the death of his father, Michelangelo penned a series of poems bemoaning his loss. Among them was this:

> But who is the man who would not cry
> For his dear father dead, not seeing again
> Him whom he saw infinite times, or many?
>
> For our intensest sorrow and our pain
> Are great or small as felt, in any person;
> Lord, what they do in me you understand.

Lionardo sent Michelangelo gifts of sausages and linen shirts, beans, cloth, and wine. In return, from his comfortable home in the unfashionable neighborhood of Macel de' Corvi, Michelangelo sent Lionardo and his other surviving relatives a stream of letters, not a few of which complained of their lack of respect for him and his work, their financial indiscretions, and their demands for help of one kind or another. Yet, though he might chide and admonish, he clearly treasured his family and supported his father, his brothers, and his nephew financially throughout his life.

Michelangelo felt the loss of his father keenly. Lodovico died in 1531, while Michelangelo was still living in Florence. Although father and son had fought over money and family, there was no doubting the depth of their mutual affection. The father's death inspired the son to compose a series of poems.

Although he longed for Florence, Michelangelo found his best friendships in Rome. But his friends, like his family, were not getting any younger. In the fall of 1546, Luigi del Riccio, who had nursed Michelangelo through a severe illness, died. The next year, a month after Michelangelo was named architect of St. Peter's, Vittoria Colonna died. Beset by a deep, penetrating grief, Michelangelo again turned to writing poetry, reflecting on Colonna's life as a blessing in his own:

> But Heaven has taken away from me the splendor
> Of the great fire that burned and nourished me;
> I am left to be a coal, covered and burning,
>
> And if Love will not offer me more timber
> To raise a fire, in me there will not be
> A single spark, all into ashes turning.

Not surprisingly, with his friends dying and his own health precarious, Michelangelo turned to thoughts of his mortality. Years earlier, people had marveled that Michelangelo could still work with remarkable vigor and accuracy. As a contemporary reported:

> *I have seen Michelangelo, although more than sixty years old and no longer among the most robust, knock off more chips of a very hard marble in a quarter of an hour than three young stone carvers could have done in three or four, an almost incredible thing to one who has not seen it; and I thought the whole work would fall to pieces because he moved with such impetuosity and fury, knocking to the floor large chunks three and four fingers thick with a single blow so precisely aimed that if he had gone even minimally further than necessary, he risked losing it all.*

By the time of Colonna's death, the sculptor, seventy-two, felt his age. "I am an old man," he wrote that year, "and death has robbed me of the dreams of my youth." Immersed in thoughts of mortality, he began work on what would become known as the *Florentine Pietà*, a piece that he intended to be placed on his own tomb. The project, eventually abandoned by Michelangelo, depicts Nicodemus, Mary, and Mary Magdalene supporting the dead body of Jesus. Nicodemus's face is a self-portrait.

The *Florentine Pietà* never made it on to Michelangelo's tomb; it is now housed in the Museo dell'Opera del Duomo in Florence.

Michelangelo worked on the *Florentine Pietà* in solitude. One night Pope Julius III sent Vasari to the artist's home, where he found Michelangelo at work on the *Pietà* by candlelight. When Vasari came into the room, Michelangelo "let the lantern drop from his hand leaving them in the dark." "I am so old," the artist said, "that death often tugs me by the cape to go along with him, and one day, just like this lantern, my body will fall and the light of life will be extinguished."

In 1548, Michelangelo's brother Giovansimone died. But probably a greater blow was inflicted in 1555, when Pietro Urbino, Michelangelo's servant and assistant for more than twenty-five years, became gravely ill. The two men had developed a familial relationship over the years, and Michelangelo nursed his friend to the end. Urbino left behind a widow and two sons. Michelangelo was

godfather to one of the boys, and he took responsibility for the entire family when Urbino died. He provided for them, invested money for them, and continued to look after them even after Cornelia, Urbino's wife, remarried.

After Urbino's death, Michelangelo wrote to his nephew of his "intense grief, leaving me so stricken and troubled that it would have been easier to have died with him." That grief, powerful and personal, may have inspired Michelangelo to begin his last sculpture, the *Rondanini Pietà*, which is in the Castello Slovzesco in Milan. Like the *Florentine Pietà*, this too is unfinished, yet beautiful and intimate. Unlike the *Rome Pietà*, which portrays Mary grieving over the body of her son in repose, the *Rondanini Pietà* is a composition of tension and balance. Mary stands on a rock struggling to hold the limp body of Jesus. There is tension in her precariousness, yet, like the *Rome Pietà*, the mother struggles to keep the body of her beloved son from the floor. Michelangelo, who lost his mother when he was six, returned again and again to sculpt and paint mothers holding and loving their children.

A Sonnet from 1554

> *My course of life already has attained,*
> *Through stormy seas, and in a flimsy vessel,*
> *The common port, at which we land to tell*
> *All conduct's cause and warrant, good or bad,*
>
> *So that the passionate fantasy, which made*
> *Of art a monarch for me and an idol,*
> *Was laden down with sin, now I know well,*
> *Like what all men against their will desired.*
>
> *What will become, now, of my amorous thoughts,*
> *Once gay and vain, as toward two deaths I move,*
> *One known for sure, the other ominous?*
>
> *There's no painting or sculpture now that quiets*
> *The soul that's pointed toward that holy Love*
> *That on the cross opened Its arms to take us.*

The elderly sculptor had the means to return to Florence at any time, but Rome kept him captive to the end. Yet, he was a willing captive. Michelangelo suffered from kidney stones and colic in his old age—both of which gave him an excuse to stay in Rome, where he could supervise the construction of St. Peter's.

In 1555, he wrote: "I am at the twenty-fourth hour, and not a thought arises in me that doesn't have death carved in it." Yet he would live nine more years, until the age of eighty-nine—extraordinary in a society where fifty was considered elderly. In 1560, Vasari reported to Duke Cosimo de' Medici, the ruler of Florence, "He now goes about very little, and has become so old that he gets little rest, and has declined so much that I believe he will only be with us for a short while, if he is not kept alive by God's goodness for the sake of the works at St. Peter's which certainly need him."

Michelangelo lived in his home at ❶ **Macel de' Corvi** until the end, surrounded by friends and occasionally visited by his nephew, who stood to inherit a sizable fortune from his childless uncle. The artist, who continued working, retained one or two assistants, a male secretary, a cook, and a housemaid. They all lived in his home and provided company as well as their

Rome's Wedding Cake

Macel de' Corvi, the "Slaughterhouse of the Crows," was in Michelangelo's time an undistinguished neighborhood filled with homes, shops, and churches. The landscape changed in the late nineteenth century, however, when work began on an enormous civic project, the ❷ **Monument to Vittorio Emanuele II.**

The monument, which was completed in 1911, emulates the architecture of the Renaissance and honors Vittorio Emanuele II, who ruled a unified kingdom of Italy from 1861 to 1868. His reign was far less pristine and harmonious than the monument, but the building expresses many of the ideals of humanism, honoring Italian history with a commemoration of civic service and a nod to ancient Roman design. In World War II, American soldiers in Rome nicknamed the it "the wedding cake," and the name stuck.

Today the Monument to Vittorio Emanuele II is the dominant feature in what was Michelangelo's neighborhood, Macel de' Corvi.

services. Pope Pius IV and Duke Cosimo visited him regularly, and their minions watched over him as well. Pierluigi Gaeta, Michelangelo's friend and aide, brought regular reports from St. Peter's.

Despite the danger that his celebrity and frailty might make him an easy target for thieves and fraudsters, Michelangelo was fully confident that those helping him were competent and trustworthy. In August 1563, he wrote to Lionardo, reassuring his anxious heir that no one was taking advantage of him.

I see from your letter that you are trusting certain envious, paltry fellows, who are writing you many lies, since they cannot twist or rob me. They are a gang of gluttons, and you are so silly you consider them trustworthy on my affairs, as if I were a child. Remove them from your presence, since they are envious scandalmongers and evil livers. As for being miserable because of the way I am being looked after and the other things you write me, I tell you I couldn't be living better, nor more faithfully looked after in everything; as for being robbed by the one I think you mean, I tell you I have people I can trust and be at peace with in the house. So attend to living, and don't think of my affairs, because I know how to watch out for myself if I have to, and am not a child. Keep well.

Farewell

By January 1564, Michelangelo was dictating his letters because "my hand no longer serves me." Yet he was still sculpting. He willed his soul to God, his body to the earth, and his possessions to his relatives in a last testament of just three sentences. On February 12, while working on the *Rondanini Pietà*, he became feverish. He spent hours burning piles of sketches and

Daniele da Volterra

One of Michelangelo's students and a loyal friend, Daniele da Volterra executed many of his paintings based on sketches by Michelangelo. ❸ **Trinità dei Monti**, the church at the top of the Spanish Steps and just steps away from the Villa Medici, holds two of Volterra's works, *Deposition* and *The Assumption*, both of which show the influence of Michelangelo's teaching. *The Assumption* includes a portrait of Michelangelo.

Bernini's father designed the fountain at the foot of the Spanish Steps, which are so called because the Spanish embassy is on the piazza.

drawings. Even in his final days, Michelangelo was conscious of his reputation and did not want to leave behind anything he did not deem perfect or worthy.

On February 15, he sent for Lionardo. His friends gathered. Daniele da Volterra and Tommaso de'

Cavalieri were among the loyal attendants who read to Michelangelo and retold, at his request, the story of Christ's crucifixion over and over again. Michelangelo lay by the fire, and eventually moved to his bed. He turned to Volterra at one point and pleaded, "O Daniele, I am done for; I am in your keeping. Do not

Bernini: Michelangelo's Heir

Born after Michelangelo's death, sculptor and architect Gian Lorenzo Bernini (1598–1680) is widely considered the finest Roman artist of the seventeenth century. He designed the Piazza San Pietro and the *baldacchino* in St. Peter's, and his gifts as a sculptor rivaled those of Michelangelo.

The son of an artist, Bernini grew up in an environment that celebrated sculpture. Bernini went on to design the enormous fountains in the ❹ **Piazza Navona.** Once an ancient racetrack, the piazza holds three fountains that testify to the Roman reverence for water. Bernini's figures also pay homage to Michelangelo's—twisting, powerful, and muscular.

The Villa Borghese, once a private estate, now has several fine museums located in a vast park area. The ❺ **Galleria Borghese** holds several of Bernini's finest sculptures. *David*, a self-portrait, takes yet another look at the ideas of strength, valor, and honor that Michelangelo explored in his own *David*. With the *Rape of Persephone* and *Apollo and Daphne*, Bernini executes two tales

from mythology with the same kind of reverence and passion and the same ability to capture in stone a sense of movement and moment that Michelangelo captures in *Moses*. Just as Moses is about to rise, so Daphne is in the midst of transformation and Persephone is captured in the moment of terrified realization. The museum also features the collection of one of Rome's great art aficionados, Scipione Caffarelli Borghese (1576–1633). The favorite nephew of Pope Paul V, Borghese collected fine examples of ancient art as well as works by contemporary geniuses, including Bernini, Caravaggio, and Rubens.

The Galleria Borghese.

The church of Santi Apostoli, where Michelangelo's body lay in state, is part of the Palazzo Colonna complex in Rome, just blocks from Michelangelo's home in Macel de' Corvi.

abandon me." Not only did Volterra stay by Michelangelo's side to the end, but he assumed his friend's mantle after his passing, taking on the responsibility of painting clothes and drapes on many of the nudes in *The Last Judgment.*

On February 18, 1564, Michelangelo's doctor wrote to Duke Cosimo in Florence, saying, "This afternoon that most excellent and true miracle of nature, Messer Michelangelo Buonarroti passed from this to a better life."

"Father and Master of Everyone"

Rome grieved deeply when Michelangelo died. His body was moved to the ❻ **church of Santi Apostoli,** adjacent to Palazzo Colonna and a few blocks from his home. The very public funeral was "attended by the entire artistic profession, as well as all his friends." Vasari recounts that "Michelangelo was buried in a tomb in the church of the Santi Apostoli in the presence of all of Rome, while His Holiness planned to erect a special memorial and a tomb in Saint Peter's itself." Michelangelo had expressed his desire to be buried in Florence, however, not in Rome. His friends knew, though, that the Romans would not let him go easily. So, unlike the public fanfare accompanying his interment in the church of Santi Apostoli, his body was moved to Florence two weeks later in secrecy, "shipped like merchandise in a bale . . . so that in Rome there would be no chance of creating an uproar." Florence welcomed her native son, and again Michelangelo's life was celebrated in elaborate style, this time in the church of Santa Croce. The Florentine Fine Arts Academicians posthumously elected Michelangelo "prime academic"—"head, father and master of everyone."

Giorgio Vasari, who played such a role in immortalizing Michelangelo on paper, designed his tomb and prepared the decorations for his memorial service. Romans may have felt betrayed. The promised memorial and tomb for Michelangelo at St. Peter's was never built, but a small memorial was installed in the courtyard of the monastery next door to Santi Apostoli.

In the days that followed Michelangelo's death, an inventory was taken of his home. His friends and relatives understood the value of his works, and they wanted to make sure nothing disappeared. The inventory records that

Giorgio Vasari designed Michelangelo's tomb in Florence's Santa Croce.

Michelangelo was at work on three large marbles: one of St. Peter, one of Christ with a cross, and the *Rondanini Pietà*. It also reveals some intimate details of Michelangelo's home life. In the room where he slept were a straw bed, a canopy of white cloth, "a long fur coat of wolf skin, old; a rough woolen lion-colored blanket, heavily used; another fur coat, half length, of wolf, with a cover of black cloth; a mantle of fine black Florentine material, with sections of black lining inside, almost new . . . a rose undershirt with a rose silk border, heavily used . . . a pale-colored undershirt with a border of the same material, heavily used."

The inventory makes no mention of any books, paintings, sculptures, or drawings that were not religious in nature. Perhaps the influence of Savonarola lingered on, and Michelangelo's burning of papers before his death amounted to his own bonfire of the vanities. The sculptor did not burn everything, however. Of the correspondence that survived, 480 letters in Michelangelo's own hand provide a testament to his life and his friendships. Hundreds more from friends, relatives, popes, and kings bear witness to his influence and personal connections across social and political strata as well as geographical boundaries. Additionally, contracts, legal statements, poems, and

notebooks, together with the testimony of his friends and biographers, create a portrait of an artist who was well loved and profoundly respected. Although he was cautious during his life about committing his political allegiances to paper, his surviving correspondence attests to his tremendous loyalty to the people whom he cherished—and venom for those he did not respect.

For his family, Michelangelo invested well. He had lived a simple but comfortable life and left enough to allow his family to do the same. Lionardo was his sole heir, and Lionardo's descendents kept the Buonarroti family line alive until the nineteenth century. In 1858, Cosimo Buonarroti, one of the last of the line, donated Michelangelo's Florence house (one that he owned but never occupied) and its contents to the city of Florence. Casa Buonarroti is now a museum and archive open to the public.

Michelangelo's greatest legacy, however, is in the marble and plaster he transformed. This bequest of beauty and grace has shaped not only the appearance of Rome but also the experience of Rome for the countless millions who have lived in and visited the city since that "true miracle of nature" departed from it.

After Michelangelo's body was removed from Santi Apostoli in Rome, a small memorial was erected. It has subsequently been enclosed in the courtyard of the church's monastery next door, but a polite inquiry about Michelangelo will generally gain admission.

Timeline

March 6, 1475 — Michelangelo Buonarroti is born in Caprese, near Florence.

December 6, 1481 — Michelangelo's mother, Francesca, dies.

April 1488 — Thirteen-year-old Michelangelo is officially apprenticed to Domenico Ghirlandaio, the Florentine master.

c. 1490 — Michelangelo leaves Ghirlandaio's studio to work in the Medici Gardens.

April 8, 1492 — Michelangelo's patron, Lorenzo de' Medici, dies, leaving the young sculptor's future uncertain.

1495 — Michelangelo catches the eye of Lorenzo di Pierfrancesco de' Medici with a work of art—a sleeping cupid. With help, he sells the piece as an antiquity. The deception is discovered, but Michelangelo uses letters from his patron to secure his first position in Rome.

June 25, 1496 — Michelangelo arrives in Rome for the first time.

1496–7 — Michelangelo creates *Bacchus*, a work that fails to please his patron, Cardinal Riario, but does secure his next commission.

1498–9 — Michelangelo works on the *Rome Pietà*, the piece that cements his reputation in Rome.

1501–4 — Michelangelo completes *David* and installs it in Florence.

November 1, 1503 — Giuliano della Rovere is elected Pope Julius II.

1505–45 — Through contract disputes, money negotiations, and vast disappointment, Michelangelo works on Julius II's tomb. When it is finally installed in 1545, the tomb bears little resemblance to the original plans.

January 14, 1506 — *Laocoön* is discovered in Rome, shaping Michelangelo's work both in stone and in paint.

April 1506 — Pope Julius II lays the cornerstone for the new St. Peter's Basilica, having engaged Bramante as the building's first architect.

1506–8 — To appease Julius II after an argument about money, Michelangelo completes a bronze statue of the pope for the city of Bologna. Citizens angry with the pope later melt the statue.

May 10, 1508–October 31, 1512 — Michelangelo works on the Sistine Chapel ceiling. The project is fraught with conflict and struggle, but the results are hailed as miraculous.

February 21, 1513 — Pope Julius II dies. In the following months, Pope Leo X, a Medici pope, is elected to replace him.

1515–34 — With Leo X as a patron, Michelangelo returns to Florence.

1518–21 — Michelangelo completes *The Risen Christ* in Florence and ships it to Rome, where his assistants install it.

May 6, 1527 —The armies of the Holy Roman Empire invade Rome, killing thousands of Romans and scarring the city for years.

1531 — Michelangelo's father, Lodovico, dies in Florence.

1532 — Michelangelo meets Tommaso de' Cavalieri. Their friendship lasts the rest of Michelangelo's life.

1534 — Michelangelo leaves Florence, which has become an unfriendly place for republicans, never to return.

1536–41 — Michelangelo returns to the Sistine Chapel, this time to paint *The Last Judgment* on the wall over the altar. Controversy about the fresco follows him until his death.

1536 — Michelangelo, working on *The Last Judgment*, meets Vittoria Colonna, a friend with whom he engages in spiritual and theological debates.

1538 — Pope Paul III engages Michelangelo to restore the Campidoglio, making the Capitoline Hill once again the heart of Rome.

1542–50 — Pope Paul III commissions Michelangelo's last frescoes. The aging artist takes nearly eight years to finish two works in the Pauline Chapel.

1546 — Michelangelo takes over the Palazzo Farnese project and is appointed chief architect of St. Peter's after the death of Antonio da Sangallo.

1547–55 — Michelangelo creates the *Florentine Pietà*. Although it was intended for his own tomb, it never was installed there.

1550 — Giorgio Vasari publishes *Lives of the Painters, Sculptors, and Architects*, which includes the first published biography of Michelangelo.

1553 — Ascanio Condivi publishes *The Life of Michelangelo,* considered more accurate than Vasari's book.

c. 1556–64 — An elderly Michelangelo works on the *Rondanini Pietà*, his last sculpture. He does not finish it before he dies.

c. 1560 — Pope Pius IV commissions Michelangelo to design the Sforza Chapel in Santa Maria Maggiore.

1561 — Michelangelo designs the church of Santa Maria degli Angeli to occupy the *frigidarium* of the Baths of Diocletian; he also designs the Porta Pia, a new gate for the Roman city wall.

February 18, 1564 — Michelangelo dies in his home at Macel de' Corvi in Rome, surrounded by friends.

Notes

Chapter 1

3: "[God] sent . . .": Giorgio Vasari, *The Lives of the Artists*, translated by Julia Bondanella and Peter Bondanella (New York: Oxford, 1998), 414.

7: "The magnificent man . . .": Quoted in Jerry Brotton, *The Renaissance Bazaar* (New York: Oxford University Press, 2002), 150.

10: "Avaricious and grasping . . .": Quoted in James Beck, *Three Worlds of Michelangelo* (New York: Norton, 1999), 94.

11: "Well built . . .": Ascanio Condivi, *The Life of Michelangelo*, translated by Alice Sedgwick Wohl (University Park: Pennsylvania State University Press, 2003), 208.

Chapter 2

15: "I record that on this day . . ." Quoted in George Bull, *Michelangelo: A Biography* (New York: St. Martin's Press, 1995), 9.

16: "If I have any . . .": Vasari, *Lives of the Artists*, 415.

19: "Although he profited . . .": Condivi, *Life of Michelangelo*, 9.

19: "go off to the fish market . . .": Condivi, *Life of Michelangelo*, 9–10.

21: "Buonarroti had the habit . . .": Benvenuto Cellini, *The Autobiography of Benvenuto Cellini*, translated by George Bull (London: Folio Society, 1970), 42.

21: "Oh, you have made . . .": Condivi, *Life of Michelangelo*, 9.

21: "If you buried . . .": Vasari, *Lives of the Artists*, 423.

21: "did not recognize . . .": Vasari, *Lives of the Artists*, 423.

25: "As the admirable . . .": Vasari, *Lives of the Artists*, 474.

Chapter 3

30: "And I tell you . . .": Matthew 16:18–19 (New International Version).

31: "found it so . . .": Brotton, *The Renaissance Bazaar*, 106.

35: "the receptacle of . . .": Quoted in Beck, *Three Worlds*, 94.

36: "On Sunday the Cardinal came . . .": Quoted in Bull, *Michelangelo: A Biography*, 34.

38: "He was very intimate . . .": Condivi, *Life of Michelangelo*, 17.

39: "looks drunken, brutal, and . . .": Harry Buxton Forman, *The Works of Percy Bysshe Shelley in Verse and Prose*, vol. 7 (London: Reeves and Turner, 1880).

39: "The sculptor in creating . . .": Quoted in William E. Wallace, *Michelangelo: The Complete Sculpture, Painting, Architecture* (Westport, Conn.: Hugh Lauter Levin Associates, 1998), 13.

40: Michelangelo worked on . . .: From G. M. Helms, "The Materials and Techniques of Italian Renaissance Sculpture," in *Looking at Italian Renaissance Sculpture*, edited by Sarah Blake McHam (Cambridge: Cambridge University Press, 1998), 20.

40: Sonnet is from Michelangelo Buonarroti, *Complete Poems and Selected Letters of Michelangelo*, translated by Creighton Gilbert and edited by Robert Linscott (Princeton, N.J.: Princeton University Press, 1980), 28.

40: "helmet made of pasteboard . . .": Vasari, *Lives of the Artists*, 475.

42: "I Jacopo Gallo . . .": Quoted in Linda Murray, *Michelangelo: His Life, Work and Times* (New York: Thames and Hudson, 1984), 20.

Chapter 4

54: "On Holy Saturday . . .": *Complete Poems and Letters*, 191.

55: "Forgive me . . .": Condivi, *Life of Michelangelo*, 35–38.

57: "No sooner had [Michelangelo pulled] . . .": Vasari, *Lives of the Artists*, 426–37.

57: "I know nothing . . .": Vasari, *Lives of the Artists*, 438.

58: "I say and affirm . . .": *Complete Poems and Selected Letters*, 264.

59: "I find I have . . .": *Complete Poems and Selected Letters*, 260.

60: "This statue alone . . .": Condivi, *Life of Michelangelo*, 77.

60: "No block of marble . . .": Michelangelo Buonarroto, *Michelangelo: Life, Letters, and Poetry*, translated by George Bull and Peter Porter (New York: Oxford University Press, 1999), 153.

61: "One who knows . . .": Quoted in Beck, *Three Worlds of Michelangelo*, 159.

Chapter 5

63: "Until you have seen . . .": John Wolfgang von Goethe, *Italian Journey*, translated by W. H. Auden and Elizabeth Meyer (New York: Schocken, 1968).

63: "Sixtus drove the darkness away . . .": Quoted in *Michelangelo and Raphael in the Vatican* (Vatican City: Ufficio Vendita Pubblicazioni e Riproduzioni dei Musei Vaticani, 1995), 16.

65: "Holy Father . . .": Beck, *Three Worlds of Michelangelo*, 176–77.

70: "realized that Michelangelo . . .": Condivi, *Life of Michelangelo*, 57.

70: "In the upper part . . .": Quoted in Murray, *Michelangelo*, 59.

70: "While he was painting . . .": Condivi, *Life of Michelangelo*, 57.

72: "He constantly wore boots . . .": Vasari, *Lives of the Artists*, 481.

72: "To make it short . . .": *Complete Poems and Selected Letters*, 202.

72: "Attend to living . . .": *Complete Poems and Selected Letters*, 206.

72: "On another occasion . . .": Vasari, *Lives of the Artists*, 450.

72: "declaring that such acts . . .": Vasari, *Lives of the Artists*, 450.

72: "When it satisfies me . . .": Vasari, *Lives of the Artists*, 442.

73: "if he were really bad . . .": *Complete Poems and Selected Letters*, 208.

73: "I said to myself . . .": quoted in Murray, *Michelangelo*, 63.

73: Sonnet to John: *Complete Poems and Selected Letters*, 5.

75: "The opinion . . .": Condivi, *Life of Michelangelo*, 57.

75: "This greatly disturbed . . .": Condivi, *Life of Michelangelo*, 57.

75: "I work harder . . .": Quoted in Murray, *Michelangelo*, 66.

77: "It will look poor . . .": Condivi, *Life of Michelangelo*, 58.

Chapter 6

81: "the knees of that figure . . .": Quoted in William E. Wallace, "Michelangelo's Risen Christ," *Sixteenth Century Journal* 28(4): 1251.

84: "I live here in great . . .": *Complete Poems and Selected Letters*, 207.

84: Sonnet to Tommaso de' Cavalieri: *Complete Poems and Selected Letters*, 51.

85: "If it is really true . . .": *Complete Poems and Selected Letters*, 253.

85: "I promise you . . .": Quoted in Murray, *Michelangelo*, 154.

86: "I have often heard . . .": Condivi, *Life of Michelangelo*, 105.

87: "a poor man . . .": Quoted in Beck, *Three Worlds of Michelangelo*, 10.

87: Madrigal to Vittoria Colonna: *Complete Poems and Selected Letters*. 131.

89: "I have wished to . . .": *Complete Poems and Selected Letters*, 268.

89: "I have had this desire . . .": Vasari, *Lives of the Artists*, 460.

91: Known to be a shabby dresser . . .: This anecdote is from Vasari, *Lives of the Artists*, 477.

91: "In desperate shape . . .": Vasari, *Lives of the Artists*, 462.

93: "Is it possible . . .": Quoted in Murray, *Michelangelo*, 161.

93: "some of the drawings . . .": Quoted in Murray, *Michelangelo*, 162.

94: "The evil, foolish . . .": *Complete Poems and Selected Letters*, 57.

95: "school for artists . . .": Bull, *Michelangelo: A Biography*, 295.

95: "Oh, how many men . . .": Quoted in Marchia B. Hall, editor, *Michelangelo's "Last Judgment"* (Cambridge: Cambridge University Press, 2005), 33.

95: "Tell the pope . . .": Quoted in Murray, *Michelangelo*, 166.

97: "Painting is to be . . .": *Complete Poems and Selected Letters*, 282.

Chapter 7

106: "I behold this noble . . .": Quoted in Bull, *Michelangelo: A Biography*, 119.

108: "If Titian . . .": Vasari, *Lives of the Artists*, 501.

Chapter 8

113: "I call God to witness . . .": *Complete Poems and Selected Letters*, 310.

116: "disegno angelico": Quoted in William L. MacDonald, *The Pantheon* (Cambridge, Mass.: Harvard University Press, 1976), 133.

117: "after the pagan filth . . .": Quoted in MacDonald, *The Pantheon*, 14.

118: "It is certain . . .": Quoted in Charles De Tolnay, *The Art and Thought of Michelangelo*, translated by Nan Buranelli (New York: Pantheon, 1964), 91.

121: "Why does not . . .": Quoted in Brotton, *The Renaissance Bazaar*, 109.

123: "The circle he puts . . .": *Complete Poems and Selected Letters*, 271.

124: "On the matter . . .": *Complete Poems and Selected Letters*, 290.

124: "Michelangelo Buonarroti is . . .": Quoted in Murray, *Michelangelo*, 210.

126: "Columns in the colonnade . . .": from "Christmas Eve" by Robert Browning in *Christmas Eve and Easter Day* (New York: Classic Books, 2000).

126: "You are aware . . .": *Complete Poems and Selected Letters*, 315.

128: "As for how I am . . .": *Complete Poems and Selected Letters*, 312.

Chapter 9

133: "If you had with . . .": *Michelangelo: Life, Letters, and Poetry*, 156.

134: "But who is the man . . .": *Michelangelo: Life, Letters, and Poetry*, 62.

134: "But Heaven has taken . . .": *Michelangelo: Life, Letters, and Poetry*, 149.

134: "You must value . . .": Quoted in William E. Wallace, "A Week in the Life of Michelangelo," in *Looking at Italian Renaissance Sculpture*, edited by Sarah Blake McHam (Cambridge: Cambridge University Press, 1998), 210.

135: "I have seen Michelangelo . . .": Quoted in Wallace, *Michelangelo*, 28.

135: "I am an old . . .": Quoted in Leo Steinberg, *Michelangelo's Last Paintings* (New York: Oxford University Press, 1975), 42.

136: "I am so old . . .": Vasari, *Lives of the Artists*, 479.

136: "I am at the twenty-fourth . . .": *Michelangelo: Life, Letters, and Poetry*, 303.

136: "He now goes about . . .": Quoted in Wallace, *Michelangelo*, 29.

136: "My course of life . . .": *Michelangelo: Life, Letters, and Poetry*, 159.

138: "I see . . .": *Michelangelo: Life, Letters, and Poetry*, 316–17.

138: "my hand no longer . . .": Quoted in Beck, *Three Worlds of Michelangelo*, 211.

139: "O Daniele, I am done . . .": Quoted in Bull, *Michelangelo: A Biography*, 413.

140: "This afternoon that . . .": Quoted in Wallace, *Michelangelo*, 29.

140: "attended by the entire . . .": Vasari, *Lives of the Artists*, 482.

141: "shipped like merchandise . . .": Vasari, *Lives of the Artists*, 482.

141: "head, father and . . .": Beck, *Three Worlds of Michelangelo*, 3.

142: "a long fur coat . . .": Beck, *Three Worlds of Michelangelo*, 221–22.

For Further Reading

Jerry Brotton, *The Renaissance Bazaar* (New York: Oxford University Press, 2002).

James Beck, *Three Worlds of Michelangelo* (New York: Norton, 1999).

George Bull, *Michelangelo: A Biography* (New York: St. Martin's, 1995).

Michelangelo Buonarroto, *Complete Poems and Selected Letters of Michelangelo,* translated by Creighton Gilbert (Princeton, N.J.: Princeton University Press, 1980).

Michelangelo Buonarroto, *Michelangelo: Life, Letters, and Poetry,* translated by George Bull and Peter Porter (New York: Oxford University Press, 1999).

Benvenuto Cellini, *The Autobiography of Benvenuto Cellini,* translated by George Bull (London: Folio Society, 1970).

Ascanio Condivi, *The Life of Michelangelo,* translated by Alice Sedgwick Wohl (University Park: Pennsylvania State University Press, 2003).

Charles De Tolnay, *The Art and Thought of Michelangelo,* translated by Nan Buranelli (New York: Pantheon, 1964).

Pieluigi De Vecchi, ed., *The Sistine Chapel: A Glorious Restoration* (New York: Abradale, 1999).

Marcia B. Hall, ed., *Michelangelo's "Last Judgment"* (Cambridge: Cambridge University Press, 2005).

Ross King, *Michelangelo and the Pope's Ceiling* (New York: Penguin, 2003).

Linda Murray, *Michelangelo: His Life, Work and Times* (New York: Thames and Hudson, 1984).

Loren Partridge, et al., *Michelangelo—The Last Judgment: A Glorious Restoration* (New York: Abradale, 2000).

J. H. Plumb, ed., *The Italian Renaissance* (New York: Houghton Mifflin, 2001).

Steffi Roettgen, *Italian Frescoes: The Flowering of the Renaissance,* translated by Russell Stockman (New York: Abbeville, 1996).

Giorgio Vasari, *The Lives of the Artists,* translated by Julia Bondanella and Peter Bondanella (New York: Oxford University Press, 1998).

William E. Wallace, *Michelangelo: The Complete Sculpture, Painting, Architecture* (Westport, Conn.: Hugh Lauter Levin Associates, 1998).

Index

Credits

Image on pages 2–3 copyright Adrian Beesley/ iStockphoto.com.

Image on page 4 is from the Toggenburg Bible, 1411.

Image on page 5 is from the Yorck Project.

Images on pages 8 and 115 copyright Marie-Lan Nguyen/Wikimedia Commons.

Image on page 9 copyright Darren Baker/iStockphoto.

Images on pages 11, 62–63, 64, and 71 are courtesy of the Art History/Classics Library, University of California, Berkeley.

Image on page 12 copyright Jeremy Edwards/ iStockphoto.com.

Images on pages 14–15, 17 (larger image), 49, 106–107, 119, 126, and 138 copyright iStockphoto

Images on page 18, 31, 65, 83, and 120 copyright Mary Evans Picture Library.

Images on pages 20, 24, and 73 copyright Scala/Art Resource, NY.

Images on pages 22, 38, and 96 copyright Erich Lessing/ Art Resource, NY.

Image on page 28 is from iStockphoto.

Image on page 23 copyright Giorgio Fochesato/ iStockphoto.

Images on pages 29, 53, and 130–131 copyright Hedda Gjerpen/iStockphoto.

Image on page 32 copyright Javarman/Dreamstime.com.

Image on pages 34–35 is from *Liber Chronicarum* (or *Nuremberg Chronicle*), folios LVIIv-LVIIIr (Morse Library, Beloit College).

Images on pages 41 and 44–45 copyright Mary Evans/ Deagostini Editore.

Images on pages 47, 55, 78–79, 85, 90, 92, and 93 copyright Alinari/Art Resource, NY.

Image on page 52 copyright William Phillips/ iStockphoto.

Image on page 57 copyright Alessandro Zingone.

Image on page 68 is by Kim Rusch.

Image on pages 76–77 copyright Asier Villafranca/ Dreamstime.com.

Image on page 88 courtesy of the Archives of the Evangelical Lutheran Church of America.

Image on page 94 copyright Giovanni Dall'Orto.

Image on page 98–99 copyright Javier García Blanco/ iStockphoto.

Image on page 101 copyright Iofoto/Dreamstime.com.

Image on pages 112–113 copyright Ihb/ Dreamstime.com.

Image on page 117 copyright Zothen/Dreamstime.com.

Image on page 125 is by Romano N. A. Nickerson.

Image on page 163 is courtesy of Jennifer L. Schum.

All other images are in the public domain or in the collection of the author.

About the Author

Angela K. Nickerson is a freelance writer and international tour guide. She travels regularly to a wide variety of countries. Married to a Roman, she enjoys visiting Italy as often as possible. She has taught writing classes and workshops for Stanford University, and is based in Sacramento, California.

About the ArtPlace Series

This book is part of the ArtPlace series published by Roaring Forties Press. Each book in the series explores how a renowned artist and a world-famous city or area helped to define and inspire each other. ArtPlace volumes are intended to stimulate both eye and mind, offering a rich mix of art and photography, history and biography, ideas and information. While the books can be used by tourists to navigate and illuminate their way through cityscapes and landscapes, the volumes can also be read by armchair travelers in search of an engrossing and revealing story.

Other titles include *A Journey into Dorothy Parker's New York*, *A Journey into Steinbeck's California*, *A Journey into the Transcendentalists' New England*, *A Journey into Flaubert's Normandy*, *A Journey into Matisse's South of France*, and *A Journey into Ireland's Literary Revival*.

Visit Roaring Forties Press's website, www.roaringfortiespress.com, for details of these and other titles, as well as to learn about upcoming author tours, readings, media appearances, and all kinds of special events and offers. Visitors to the website may also send comments and questions to the authors of ArtPlace series books.

A Journey into Michelangelo's Rome

This book is set in Goudy and Futura; the display type is Futura Condensed. The cover and the interior were designed by Jeff Urbancic, who also composed the pages. Kim Rusch designed the maps. Sherri Schultz, Nigel Quinney, and Deirdre Greene copyedited the text, which was proofread by Jean Patterson and indexed by Sonsie Conroy.